YOU VERSUS YOU

LESSONS FROM GREAT MARTIAL ARTISTS ON DEVELOPING A FIGHTING SPIRIT FOR LIFE

ADAM CORCORAN

YOU
VERSUS
YOU

First published in Ireland and Great Britain 2020 by Red Branch Incorporated.

© Copyright Adam Corcoran

The moral right of the author has been asserted.

A CIP catalogue record for this book is available from the British Library.

ISBN: 978 1 79912 019 3

CONTENTS

YOU
VERSUS
YOU

FOREWORD
BY JOHN KAVANAGH

The Four Minute Mile. It was first achieved in 1954 by Roger Bannister, at age 25, in 3 minutes and 59 seconds. I don't know how many hundreds of years athletes had been trying to break this record, but it was broken again only two months later. Since then more than 1,400 male athletes have done it. In fact, it's been lowered by almost 17 seconds. Can we explain this sudden deluge of athletes breaking a record that stood for centuries by simply pointing to the better training methods or improved nutrition? Maybe, but I don't think so. There's a huge change in psychology in humans attempting something that's never been done compared with repeating something they know has already been accomplished.

When I was part of Conor McGregor's journey towards becoming the UFC's first ever simultaneous two-weight World Champion, journalists and fans alike would constantly remind us that nobody from Ireland had come close to clinching one world title, never mind two. Conor was assured that, unless he went to America to train at one of the established training camps, he would never achieve his goals. But like Roger Bannister before him, he decided to smash that barrier in front of him. Now my gym is packed with teenagers, confident they can become the next World Champion now knowing that it IS possible.

The reason I enjoyed Adam's book so much was that I felt it released me from some mental prison cells that you might have found yourself in. Reading powerful stories about those who have gone before me and achieved so much helped reassure myself that if someone else can do it then why can't I? I hope you enjoy reading the book as much as I did and more importantly that it can nudge you onto your own path to discover just how great YOU can be.

- *John Kavanagh - Dublin, March 2020*

PREFACE
THE CAVE

We're going to start this experience out in a cave. No, not Plato's or Batman's. I mean, *the* cave, the one that everyone is talking about when we say "caveman." Now let's turn back the clocks on all of humanity, all the way until we see some of them living in that dark hole in the Earth.

We've all seen time travel movies; we know what happens when you go to the past and change even the smallest detail. Think of the massive ripple effect that would occur if we just made a minor adjustment to pre-historic civilisation. What if fire was discovered a month earlier or the idea to create tools, like the axe, struck some other great mind of the time?

A few small tweaks like that could easily set humanity on a different course. Imagine one such adjustment, then fast forward. What would be different? Well for starters, religion wouldn't exist in the same form it does today unless Jesus came down and preached again, or Muhammad re-surfaced and did his thing. We wouldn't have movies exactly like *Star Wars* and *Titanic* or TV shows such as *Friends* or *Rick and Morty*. As the ripple of change echoed through time, it would erase anything that resulted from chance, inspiration, creativity, or culture.

But, we would have scientific principles, wouldn't we? People would eventually get curious and start to study anatomy, chemistry, and physics. We would still have gravity. Light would still travel at the same speed. Someone would have the honour of being the first to discover a planet, someone else would be the first to look at a single cell under a microscope. Science is objective and constant.

In terms of human nature and psychology, the same thing applies to martial arts. At a basic level, we need self-defence. We need to fight. Like the president of the

Ultimate Fighting Championship (UFC), Dana White says, "Fighting is in our DNA. We get it, and we like it."

From the gladiators in Ancient Rome to Olympic sports like Tae Kwon Do, Wrestling, and Judo, to today's Mixed Martial Arts events, fighting is a part of us. Just as the speed of light is woven into the fabric of the universe, martial arts and the need to fight are woven into our minds.

We deal with conflict every day. In today's society, mental and emotional conflict are more prevalent than physical fights, unless you count dragging yourself out of bed to be that kind of fight. No matter how you define it, conflict is simply a part of our lives.

We are currently the most virtually connected we've ever been, but we're also the most emotionally disconnected. Many people feel as though life is constantly bringing them down. People in our generation have become disconnected from the lives that they want to live, from their childhood aspirations. The effect of this disconnect is an incredibly pissed off and miserable population.

Occurrences of depression and anxiety are at an all-time high, despite this being the most prosperous period in history. We hang around people we don't like, working jobs we hate, getting more progressively disheartened by each paycheck. If we look at it in the wrong light, we can start to feel as though life is this five-hundred-pound monster sitting on our chest.

This state of the world has resulted in an increased outcry for help. The emotional economy of humankind is changing. So, what's the supply that answers this new demand? Self-help books. We're inundated with enough self-help books to beat the band. The varying forms of advice create a spectrum that's wide enough to make a rainbow jealous. Say your daily affirmations. Wish upon a star. Ask the universe to help you. Go to the craft store and make a vision board. Uncover what kind of animal you were in your past life.

This age of (mostly bullshit) self-help is fast drawing to a close because the methods don't work beyond a brief nudge from our old friend, the placebo effect. They don't solve the real problems in life. They're simply not practical.

So, that's what we're here to do: get practical. We don't need to go to the craft store, all we need to do is look deeper into the mindset that allows some people to pick up and slam a two-hundred-pound opponent to the ground. More importantly, we're here to look at the discipline that allows that same two hundred pounder to get back on their feet and keep fighting.

The common misconception is that martial arts only offer a framework for physical conflict resolution. You swing a punch at me, I duck, take-down, and choke. However, if you go back through history, the various martial arts actually offer a framework of principles for dealing with mental and emotional conflict. Yes, adopting these fighting abilities gives you an edge in any physical confrontation, but they can also help you resolve the all-out civil war raging on in your mind. Martial arts can arm us in the struggle to cope with our very lives.

One significant distinction between this book and the flood of others out there: I do not claim to be your teacher. This is not the biography of some pasty ginger kid who fancied himself to be a martial artist, climbed to greatness, and decided to send a ladder back down to you. I'm not great. We're here to meet a full cast of *way* better-qualified mentors, and I am not one of them. In fact, I'm just the student that sits one seat over from you.

Before you meet the crew and learn their ways, I'll address some questions that you've probably already thought of so far. Who the fuck is this guy and who says he can write a book about timeless martial arts principles and the lasting life lessons they offer? How is he qualified to impart centuries of martial arts wisdom into one book?

It's a solid question, so, good job asking it. I can't answer with a stacked resume or a list of certificates, and I absolutely refuse to force a dramatised autobiography on you. In fact, after this obligatory preface, there's not an autobiographical bone in this book's body. That would only serve me, not you.

To answer your question, I can only tell you my relationship to the topic at hand. You see, martial arts saved my life.

On the cusp of my mid-twenties, I found myself living in a converted cattle shed out in the arse-end of rural Ireland. I was overweight, failing my Master's degree, and working an internship for peanuts. Let's not forget the black pit of all dark days: my girlfriend at the time broke up with me over a lack of aforementioned peanuts.

I drove an ancient Nissan Micra that leaked petrol every god damn time I filled it up. Any time I drove over 60km per hour, that junk pile's relentless rattling reminded me of how truly fragile my life was. Just like that car, I was being shaken to pieces, breaking at the bolts.

Things were rough. I got depressed. Severely.

I vividly remember sitting on the floor of my converted cattle shed, darkly gazing at a length of rope on my lap. When it wasn't the rope, I would hold and quietly regard a razor blade while listening to angsty Linkin Park songs. The lyrics sang of a consuming, confusing force inside me, pulling me below the surface. For a while, that song of lacking self-control and feeling never-ending fear became my anthem.

...I know. Linkin Park. Ugh. I guess that just goes to show you how bad things really were.

I can't count how many times I thought of grabbing that rope and making a one-way trip to a secluded spot with a big tree, or making that razor blade the last thing I ever touched. I felt as though I was an observer of my own life. It was just a movie, one of those god-awful horror movies where viewers are screaming at the screen, begging an idiot character not to go into the murderer's dark basement without so much as a flashlight. I could almost hear the audience calling out to me, shouting for me to shift my life into some other direction. Depression pulled at me, though. I was being controlled, completely at the mercy of the garbage screenwriter that was dreaming up my life.

Maybe you know someone who's suffered from depression or had an anxiety attack. Chances are, it's someone close to you. Maybe it's you. You, or they, might feel compelled to write, blog, or talk about your experience to help others. That's to be encouraged; it's brave, but let's draw a very thick, important line, here:

When someone "survives" a negative mental health event, there's a temptation to tell a triumphant tale and perform an uplifting story of how they slew the great dragon of depression. You know that rags to riches story; "...started from the bottom now we here." That struggle for success against all the odds, enduring an abusive childhood, having a bitch of a mother, having a dickhead of a father, sleeping on the streets, making it off the bread line. These are real, horrible struggles, and a lot of inspiration can come from hearing about how someone overcame adversity. However, the moment those stories are reduced to fluffy, bullshit storytelling, they lose their meaning.

My journey back from the brink was propelled by martial arts. I practised Judo, MMA, Muay Thai, Boxing, and Brazilian Jiu-Jitsu as a means of therapy kind of. At the start of that journey, it was all about the *Fight Club* mentality of "hit me harder to dull the pain." I began to see that all of life's problems become background noise when some guy is either trying to break your arm or knock you unconscious.

Gradually, I progressed beyond the Brad Pitt / Edward Norton unhealthy "hurt me" angst, and *way* beyond Linkin Park lyrics. I found "my thing," and started focusing exclusively on Brazilian Jiu-Jitsu above all other martial arts. Developing a fighting spirit for life is a good way to get yourself unstuck and moving towards your most authentic aspirations and potential.

By immersing myself in martial arts, I found out just how helpful it can be in all facets of life. Sure, I learned how to twist people into human pretzels, but I also gained a more practical skillset. With an expanding ability to settle inner emotional and mental conflict, I was able to twist my own problems into pretzels, too.

Just because I learned that strength, doesn't mean I'm qualified to teach it. Why make myself a middle man when I can simply point you to the true masters? I did not write this book because I feel that I have attained some wisdom and now feel qualified to preach. I did all of this typing because this is the book that I wish existed when I was swimming in my own personal abyss. The simple act of writing it helped me get through those tough times. Maybe it will help you, too.

This book relies on current biographies and historical examples, instead of my personal life. There is a little discussion from my side to spark some reflections of your own circumstances, but I have tried mainly to arrange these pages so that you can arrive in the same headspace I did when I finished writing it. That is, you'll develop a combative attitude, a fighting spirit to help you with your problems. You will obtain the freedom to accomplish those life-changing goals you've set out to achieve.

So, just think of me as the aggregator, the one who put all the lessons in one place so you can learn them in your own way. From here on out, there will be no more angst, no more Linkin Park songs, just encounters with some of the greats and stories of what made them who they are.

It's time to fight back against the bullshit.

- Adam Corcoran - Dublin, December 2019

INTRODUCTION

You. Are. So. Fucked.

There's a 500-pound monster named Life, sitting on your chest, pinning you to the ground. Its insane weight is crushing sweet air from your wheezy lungs as it drools on your face, laughing at you.

You didn't ask for this.

You didn't want to be smothered, smack bang in the middle of two giant, disgustingly sweaty boobs, trying desperately to get out. As if having your very existence crushed out of your lungs isn't enough, this monster called Life is free to punch you in the face whenever it wants. You're in its court, at its mercy.

Is this really how the fight has to go? Some people think so, because its an easy assessment. Big should always beat small, right? Sometimes, the matchup isn't fair. It's not the kind of fight that's regulated by rules and referees. There are no weight classifications, cages, or points systems.

What you may not realise is that this total lack of rules can work in favour of both combatants. You can change the fight, level the playing ground. What if this beast on top of you wasn't so heavy? What if the boobs weren't so sweaty? What if you could leverage your way out from underneath this mammoth opponent and choke it out? If you could flip the switch and turn the tides on Life, what would you do?

The answer seems obvious. Flip the switch. Amazingly, when presented with the option, most people will keep doing what they've always done.

Absolutely fucking nothing.

We already know about the Fight or Flight response, inherent in all species on this planet, but there's a third option nobody ever talks about. It's a disservice to the human condition that they don't call it "Fight, Flight, Freeze," because all of us have frozen at one point in our lives. I'm not just talking about "deer in the headlights" motionless. There are some kinds of freeze that can last years, if we give in to our excuses.

We blame Obama, social media, Mom, Dad and everybody else, and everything else. Or we label ourselves losers, our aspirations as unrealistic. When really it's only our perception that's all tangled up.

I'm obligated to write this disclaimer. Sing it with me now, "Every situation is different." Some excuses are better than others. That's true, and far be it from me to belittle your situation. Luckily, I don't have to, because even though every situation is different, the emotions we experience are the same. Somewhere along the line, we all feel disconnected. Angry. Confused. Helpless. Afraid. Frustrated. Depressed.

Sound familiar?

These emotions are the common ground on which we'll be waging war against life. By attacking those weaknesses first, we'll give you a real shot at putting down this 500-pound metaphorical beast. Whatever emotions you're feeling right now, whatever is crippling you, others have felt the same before. So, rather than studying someone that conquered a problem similar to yours, we only need to find a subject that has defeated the emotional freeze.

Some people have developed reactors that are burning within them 24/7, melting away the ice. We're here to analyse them, and how they conquered the enemy that you are currently facing. In particular, I'd like to discuss the select group of people who are incredibly confident, self-assured, and able to perform half-naked in front of millions of people with no signs of pressure. No, I'm not talking about porn stars.

When you think of martial artists, you probably picture one of two things: an ancient Asian dude with a wispy beard and weird robe, or a boneheaded MMA Mongoloid dragging his knuckles on the ground. Regardless of what you think the average IQ of an MMA fighter is, they can teach us a hell of a lot about life. These people are fighters, and the most successful of them are not frozen in place. In fact, most of them are pretty successful – even outside of their chosen martial art. How do they do that? What's the secret?

There are names you'll see in this book that you've already heard of, and some of them you won't: Helio Gracie, Ronda Rousey, Vinny Paz, Danny Jacobs, Adam Wheeler, Conor McGregor, Helen Maroulis. These are the kind of people that found a way to keep their generators running, to fight the emotional freeze, to dry Life's sweaty boobs.

The point is not to know each of their life stories. It's how they overcame their personal hurdles that we're interested in. We need to understand that these people experienced the same emotions as you, dealt with the same shit you're dealing with right now. The only difference is, they cracked the code of the fight against Life.

It was their attitude that got them through these things. The ancient samurai, as with most things, have a much cooler term for this attitude. They call it the Fighting Spirit, the ability to flow with everything that is thrown in your way, or at you. Many people today have lost this fighting spirit.

The founder of Karate Gichin Funakoshi once said that every plant and animal has its own self-defence mechanism. A cat has claws; a rose has thorns, but humankind has lost its self-defence mechanism. Funakoshi said that for human's minds to focus on higher things, we first have to regain our self-defence mechanism.

Gichin wasn't just talking about defending against kicks and punches. Arguably, he would be wrong if he was talking strictly about the physical front. Our fists aren't bad, our legs are pretty strong, our teeth work alright, so if all else fails we've got some pretty deadly weapons available to us. No, he wasn't talking about that department; he was talking about life in general. No opponent we face is going to be as big as Life itself. Not all conflicts are external. Our generation is lacking a framework for coping with internal strife. This is where martial arts can help us.

Our internal struggle against life doesn't involve taking shins to the face or grappling for position against a steel fence. Life is much more subtle with its resistance. We're trying to do something major and find that our problems have a significant reach advantage on us and we're instantly out of ideas. So what do we do? We can either stay in the pocket and cut our problems off, or close the distance for a takedown.

It's simple, but simple doesn't mean easy.

There's a fuck tonne (that's metric system) of self-help books and personal development material out there that have helped us positively affirm we're in touch with the universe. They talk about declaring your perfect world and implementing big change when really, as we'll find out in this book, success in a particular area is just the basics done really well. This is not a book that tells you to have blind faith and open your chakras to connect your energy to the universe.

Whether you're having trouble getting a job, stuck in a bad relationship, or continuously at odds with uninspiring goals and self-sabotage – we can turn it into an advantage by the following martial artists' example. All great victories, not only in the cage or on the mat – involved solving problems – how you solve these problems is a measurement of how successful you'll be in life.

Our generation needs a new framework for countering Life's strikes – a fighting spirit – one that will turn this monster onto its head and twist its gigantic limbs into submission.

1

SURVIVING THE BLENDER

Before I tell you about Helio Gracie, let's put things in perspective. Saying that Gracie trained in Brazilian Jiu-Jitsu for eighty-one years is really just offering up a number. We can't fully appreciate the length of Gracie's career until we define it with historical bookends. Queen Elizabeth II was only two years old the first time Helio was exposed to Jiu-Jitsu. His final training session was ten days before his death, the year that Barak Obama was sworn in as the U.S. president.

Helio is revered as one of Brazil's first sporting heroes. He is the man that many credit for putting the "Brazilian" in Brazilian Jiu-Jitsu. Throughout his eighty-one years of devotion and discipline, he fought a vast array of world-renown martial artists such as freestyle wrestler Wladek Zbyszko and Jiu-Jitsu world champion Masahiko Kimura. Try to imagine eighty-one years of throwing and being thrown. Imagine the work that Helio had to put in, making his mind grow stronger as his body aged. (Notice I said aged, not weakened.) This guy watched the world change while sticking to one lifelong constant.

Helio's career is certainly a colossal achievement, especially given that he was a string bean of a man. He never went over 65 kilograms in weight. It came as no surprise to anyone that many of his opponents throughout his fighting career enjoyed a significant weight and reach advantage over him. It's not these David v Goliath type fights that make Helio's achievements remarkable, but rather his ability to take personal ownership of his individual situation.

You see, Helio became really good at taking fundamental responsibility of his life; this involved his Jiu-Jitsu fights, business opportunities, and ultimately his family's future. He would constantly seek to improve all of the above, simply accepting the fact that nobody was going to do these things for him.

He was a tactician of life, and only sought out battles he could act upon personally, no matter how minor the action was. If there was something Helio could do to improve his Jiu-Jitsu (and therefore his life) he was ready to do it and make good use of it. Although he willingly pushed himself fully at enormous tasks and losing battles, he also applied the same level of discipline to the small ones. Rather than throwing himself repeatedly at a metaphorical wall, he would seek out the one loose brick in the wall and pluck it, then the next, and the next. This was how he broke through the barriers that life put in front of him. Whether the goal was large or small, he was ready to give every ounce of effort and energy he had in order to make it happen. He would have preferred to die on the mat than give any less.

The seed of Helio's career was planted in 1908, when his brothers Carlos, George, and Oswaldo started training in Jiu-Jitsu under Mitsuyo Maeda, more affectionately known as Count Koma. The nickname was earned by his distinct ability to render his opponents unconscious, thereby putting them into momentary comas. Maeda was travelling the world at the time, teaching Judo and Jiu-Jitsu, fighting everybody who wanted to try him. He was, at the time, the modern version of the classic roaming samurai character. He had adopted this lifestyle as part of the Japanese policy at the time to spread their culture westwards.

There are a lot of success stories that start with someone telling the hero, "You're not good enough, kid. Go home." Helio's story is one of these. He was deemed too frail and weak to train, and was not allowed to join Maeda's class. His stature wasn't the only thing working against him. Helio also suffered from unexplainable fainting spells. A condition like that would normally spell the end of any kind of athletic aspiration, let alone a martial art.

Game over man.

Find another trough to eat in.

But...

Helio continued to show up to each and every practice led by Maeda. If he wasn't allowed to train his body, he would at least sharpen his mind. He sat off to the side and began to memorise everything, the joint locks, the throws, the chokeholds, essentially everything his brothers needed to make human pretzels out of each other.

Can you imagine the nightmare of all your brothers being taught secret ninja moves and not you? Helio's frustration must have been all-powerful. Surely, he repeatedly searched for an opportunity to be a part of this training, rather than just doing it on his own. That opportunity arose in 1920, when his brother Carlos set up his own Jiu-Jitsu school in 1920. For those of you keeping track: Yes, that is twelve years of training in secret and on the sidelines, waiting for a chance to join the community.

Carlos' students were mostly wealthy kids who wanted to learn self-defence, and most classes were taught one on one. One day, Carlos didn't show up to teach, and who was there in the school just waiting for his chance to part with some theoretical knowledge? Helio Gracie.

He taught the student one class, and from then on out, the student couldn't get enough. He asked Carlos if Helio could continue working with him, Carlos agreed.

Boom.

Foot in the door after twelve years of searching.

Helio could've pursued another, less demanding sport. He could've run a business, done anything other than the thing he was considered too weak to participate in, but Jiu-Jitsu is what he wanted to do. Despite having the deck stacked so much against him, there was still a chance for him, however minuscule it might appear today. He took it; snatching and holding on to that opportunity led to thousands of Jiu-jitsu matches and a career worth writing about.

Less than ten years later, Helio mustered up some of that same tenacity when he took on world champion Kimura, weighing in at 98 kilos to Helio's 65. Kimura publicly remarked that if this fight lasted more than three minutes, he would consider it a win for Helio. Even in the chaos of a crowd of 200,000 (including the Brazilian president), Helio remained calm and collected. Before the fight, he reminded his brothers he wouldn't give up until there was nothing left he could do.

Helio lasted thirteen minutes before being defeated in the grasp of an arm lock that would later be named after Kimura. The 65-kilogram fighter said that those thirteen minutes felt like being stuck in a blender.

The loss to Kimura could've signalled the end of Helio's career. He was 38 years old then, a healthy age to retire from fighting for any combat sports athlete. He refused to accept the "R" word. In fact, losing to Kimura was the pinnacle of Helio's technical development in terms of recognising his Jiu-Jitsu. His game was super effective against much bigger, stronger, and faster men. Helio could always hold his own.

This brings us to the reason for Helio's dedication, the driving force behind his career. As we've discussed, Helio's body, even as a boy, seemed designed for the express purpose of losing fights. Jiu-Jitsu offered him a way to negate others' superior genetics. It granted him an incredible power, and an incredible life.

He often asked his sons, who would later follow his footsteps in Jiu-Jitsu, "If a bigger man fights and smaller man to a draw. Who actually wins?" The answer he would give would always be the smaller man, because the smaller man needs more tools and, naturally, isn't supposed to defeat bigger men.

Helio continued to train and fight, and I don't just mean fight opponents. He fought against life, tooth and nail. He seemed to relish in undertaking battles in which he was outmatched, win or lose. Losing was training to Helio, perhaps his favourite kind. In 1955, he fought his former student Valdemar Santana, a fighter in his prime who was sixteen years Helio's younger. The fight went on for 3 hours 40 minutes before Santana eventually won. Put yourself in Helio's shoes. At which point did he realise he could not win? We'll never know. At which point did he give up? Never.

For our purposes, it's not the number of wins Helio had throughout his career, but the number of losses he withstood while continuing to press forward. Because of Helio taking personal responsibility, his family is worth hundreds of millions of dollars today.

We can harness the same power that Helio had. To do this, we should focus our energy on the things that are in our control, and recognise things that are not. It's a hell of a lot easier to fight life's problems when you aren't already fighting the fact that your siblings were jerks, or that a kid in pre-school made fun of you once. That stuff is ancient history. Or at least should be.

(Still, fuck that kid in pre-school).

What if you took ownership of the things that you could change in your life? That's where the real power comes in. It isn't about how you generate it, but how you spend it. Don't blast your energy against the wall, laser-focus it onto the weakest brick like Helio.

There's a great, elegant formula written by Jack Canfield that reads: E + R = O.

Event plus Response equals Outcome.

You can never change the shit that happens to you (E,) but when we change our reactions (R), we get a different outcome (O.)

So, what's our R? What's the part of the equation that is within our control?

Our emotions, perspectives, actions, and thoughts.

On the other hand, what is not up to us?

Well, you know, everything else. Weather, traffic, the Kardashians, other people's emotions, mean tweets, earthquakes, etc.

If what was up to Helio was the Jiu-Jitsu mat, then what was not up to him were the rules and conditions of the fight. Champion martial artists don't spend time arguing against the rules and regulations. They don't complain that they can't kick their downed opponent's head, or knee them in the groin. They don't say that gravity is at fault when they miss a jab or get slammed onto their back. All of those things seem like an obvious waste of energy in the context of a combat sport, but you would be surprised how much time people spend arguing with the referee of life. By the way, arguing can sometimes be classified as simply *thinking* about the things you cannot control. Thought is fucking energy, people!

We need to leverage your personal power of ownership against this huge brute of life. Helio did not believe he was better than anyone else. He believed that his techniques were insurmountable. He never fought with hate. He was always focused on what he could do. He was free from hate because he paid no frustration to things that were beyond his control. Another word for this: acceptance.

To accept life as a challenge and to make the best of it anyways, that's the choice.

What choice will you make?

2

THE DEVIL HIMSELF

He was nicknamed the Pazmanian Devil for his fast-paced nature both inside and outside the boxing ring. Occasionally, he would play to this nickname by wearing devil's horns to his matches. The man was a tornado of strength and skill. Sadly, after an incredibly successful run, Vinny Pazienza faced one of the most difficult obstacles an athlete can come up against when he broke his neck in a head-on car crash a few weeks after capturing his second boxing world title in 1991. A cage-like brace contraption called a "halo" was physically drilled into his skull. It was a brutal irony, given he used to enter the ring wearing a gown with red devil horns on it.

He asked doctors how long it would be until he could train again. They replied with a horrible prognosis. He could never box again as his spine would rupture easily. "Quiet" is not a term you'd use to describe Paz's disposition. Even when doctors told him that the break in his neck was less than a quarter of an inch from paralysing him permanently and that any further movement could leave him wheelchair-bound forever, he, well... better to let him describe it.

"I said, 'What do you mean, doc?' and that's when I started banging my legs and my arms. I literally freaked out. They had to give me a sedative to knock me out."

Vinny Panzienza's story is in this book for a reason, though, and it's not his (somewhat justified) temper tantrum. You might be able to guess where this is going. It's the ending that we all hoped *Million Dollar Baby* was heading for. But we're not just interested in the story's ending, we want to take a look at the journey.

The doctors weren't the only people trying to keep Paz out of the ring. His parents, Louise and Angelo, fought tooth and nail to keep him from doing something that, by conventional wisdom, was utterly stupid. Paz must have recognised the odd regression his life made back to high school days after being fitted with the halo. He was back to living with his parents in their Rhode Island home. In an act of youthful rebellion, he would secretly sneak down to the gym in their basement and pump weights. Paz' training wasn't going to be stopped by the clear risk of paralysis. Or even by the pain that came with that training. Okay, maybe pain is an understatement. Paz put himself through hellish agony. He recalls, "when I lifted the first weight, I picked up two dumbbells and my neck exploded. The pain shot through like a red flame of fire. I dropped the weights. I stood there for half an hour just looking at the weights and I did it again, I was screaming and crying."

Instead of completely breaking down as many would have done in such a dismal situation, Paz refused to give up on his boxing. Whether he broke his neck or not, Paz maintained that he had choices. Despite his physical incapacity, no one could take his choices away from him.

Was he pissed off about what happened him? I imagine he was, but Paz refused to let those emotions drive his life. Of course he was heartbroken with the injury but refused to hear "no." As soon as he could, he started moving again, super slowly at first and gradually built up - micro movement by micro movement. This is an important distinction; Paz didn't rebelliously rush back into training to show his body who's boss. He had the determination to train his way out of his situation, but also the discipline to do it slowly.

All of this craziness had a single purpose: Every second, every minute, was spent recovering from the injury. Paz wouldn't come back to boxing simply to make up the numbers or be a gatekeeper. He wanted to become a world champion. He'd come back bulked up, more explosive, well rounded, and better than ever.

To the amazement of doctors, rather than harming him, the illicit workouts actually aided Paz's recovery. Within six months, the halo came off. Paz added his own dash of insanity to the process when he refused to take any sedatives during the removal of the bolts that were embedded in his skull. The doctors couldn't believe his refusal as bone had actually started growing around the bolts. Paz sums up the removal of the bolts in one word: "horrific".

Another seven months passed, and Paz declared himself ready to fight. Although, "fight" in this context meant something a little different. The battle that immediately followed didn't involve fists. Paz had to convince someone to spar with him. No one wanted to be the one who accidentally put him in a wheelchair. Even when he finally found a reluctant volunteer, he couldn't get his opponent to actually try winning. Paz, unsurprisingly, got his own way.

"I sparred with a kid called Ray Oliviera. He didn't want to hit me so I started smashing him and then, of course, he began hitting me back."

Paz came back to beat former world champion Luis Santana in a tenth round decision, and went on to win two more world championship titles in 1993 and 1996. He also went on to defeat boxing legend, Roberto Duran, not once but twice. He had made his choice. He never asked for the injury to happen, but it did. That's the part that was out of his control. The only choice he had to make was to decide how it affected him; nobody else had that power to choose for him.

According to Paz, even in the hardest of times, we're never truly powerless. We don't need to break our neck for the privilege of making that strong choice. Your mind will always remain your own. Many great martial artists like Paz understand this. It's how many fighters, instead of simply overcoming disadvantages, actually transform them into strengths. Paz didn't have much physical power after his injury, but he understood that it didn't make him any less of a mental dynamo.

From this, we gain an important life principle: there is the event itself, and there is the story we tell ourselves about what we think it means. Without that story, without our perceptions, there is no good or bad. We write the story; we decide the genre. Is yours action, drama, or horror?

3

TAKE IT FROM
THE RUSSIANS

Japanese judokas utterly dominated nearly every judo competition from 1934 to 1963. That's to be expected, since Japan is the home of Judo. Surely, the creators of the style should always be vastly superior to those who adopt it, right? So what happened in 1963?

A hybrid of speed and raw power was formed, and the Soviet Union team emerged.

Their strategy of unrelenting pressure and power slams was designed to exploit the judokas, who weren't able to withstand the powerful wrestling base of the Russians. What gave the Soviets such a solid advantage? Partially, this was a matter of cultural upbringing. Many of Russia's fighters had practised some variation of grappling since they were toddlers. Some even had pet bears they would wrestle with, daily. Not a joke.

For nearly a decade after the arrival of this new Soviet power, the Japanese judo team, from players to coaches, could only see two things: the power of Soviet judo, and the Japanese' susceptibility to it. They saw an unstoppable force, which inspired in them one of the many things we seek to defeat in this book. The enemy? Hopelessness.

The first major judo competition between the Soviet Union and Japan occurred in 1963, in Kyoto, Japan. Russia's Boris Mishchenko was simply radiant with slow, confident movements as he squared off against Japanse judoka Isao Okano on the mat. He pinned his opponent within twenty seconds. This was, of course, a major upset in the world of Judo.

"As soon as the match begins, the Russian grabs the

jacket of the Japanese, drops on his back and does a
perfect armbar juji-katame. Okano taps. The whole
match lasts less than 20 seconds."

~Mark Law in his book "Falling Hard:
A Journey into the World of Judo."

What made this swift victory even more shocking and
historic was the use of a new technique. The armbar
employed by Mischenko was unknown in Japanese judo
prior to this match.

The Soviet judo team continued to grow in strength,
most notably in World championships. In 1975 the
Soviet Union closed out the 70kg division with two
Russians in the final and two Japanese players finishing
joint third. It was the first time in judo competition
history that the Japanese didn't win that division.

So what created this wave of change? Other than kids
wrestling with actual bears, I mean. As long as the
Soviets could bend but not break down on the receiving
end of the lightning-fast Japanese grips, their defence
was impenetrable and the success of their offence was

just a matter of time. If the Russians could get close, they could execute devastating hip throws or force the Japanese to react and counter them, often by throwing them over their shoulder for match-ending scores.

Russian and Japanese judo styles were completely different, the chief difference being that one was newer and more evolved. Japanese were traditional with upright postures and a technical approach, as opposed to the Russians who were maulers, brutes with strength and bullish techniques. They managed to exploit previously hidden flaws in traditional judo's very DNA.

This turning of the tides is a textbook example of how our mindset plays a role in the success or failure of our opponents. In the early sixties, before Russians gained momentum and their technique proved it could stand up to the Japanese, the Russians had to enter their matches with nothing more than belief in themselves. It's one thing to not be overwhelmed when coming up against a big powerhouse like Japan, but another thing to go out on a competition mat and perform to your peak against more experienced and supposedly vastly superior athletes as if it's just business as usual. This approach leads to a dramatic change in how we see things as opportunities as opposed to problems - the Soviets weren't looking at the problem but at the opportunity that's within it.

Yet, we're pretty fucking useless at looking at things in this way. Why? Because we don't *have* to. Imagine you're in the Soviet coach's shoes. You'll probably be exiled to some remote Gulag if the results don't come in. You *have* to get results.

Now, imagine if we absolutely *have* to achieve a goal. How different would our mindset be? Perceptions tell us things should be a certain way. When they're not as we expect them to be, we freak out and assume we've tumbled into a pitfall, when really everything is still up for grabs.

Let's look at an example everybody can relate to – working on something we absolutely hate. The spectrum of things is wide in this category. It can include doing dishes, a job, or a dissertation for college. The list goes on. All we see is hell, just like the Japanese judo team. We flinch and then get body slammed.

Take for example that dickhead in your workplace, or gym, or life—the one who causes you endless headaches. Think: they really do offer you benefits, don't they? Let's side-step to a fictional but still martial arts-related exchange that sums this up. The Joker once said to Batman, "Kill you? Why would I kill you? You complete me."

Disclaimer: I'm not encouraging you to don clown makeup and go terrorising a city, but you get the point. Your rival keeps you on your toes and encourages you, motivates you to out-perform them. They complete you. That's the power of competition. It's another example of a negative presence in your life having a positive effect, if you look for it.

 "That which doesn't kill me makes me stronger" is not a cheesy cliché, but the truth. We can either fight our problem all the way, or flip it, using its momentum in our favour just as the Soviets did with the Japanese in Judo. Either option means the problem still exists, one way just hurts a hell of a lot less.

4

THE MIRACLE MAN

At age 24, Danny Jacobs was an up and comer in the boxing world. He was one of the sport's hottest prodigies. Before he turned 25, his story of rising fame took a horrible turn, similar to that of Vinny Pazienza from chapter two.

Unbeknownst to Jacobs, while he fought and trained, a large tumour was wrapping itself around his spine. He was slowly falling into the grasp of osteosarcoma. At the height of its awful power, the tumour paralysed Jacobs from the waist down. Consigned to a wheelchair, he was told he should prepare for a life without boxing.

Through months of hospital treatment, Jacobs fought the malignant disease and emerged seventeen months later with a clean bill of health. In the ring, he earned the nickname of "The Miracle Man." Already, we can begin to see how his response to the situation turned the outcome upside down. Remember when I called him a hot young prodigy? Plenty of people have been called that in the boxing world, but there's only been one Miracle Man.

Spinal injuries are one example of the disasters that athletic careers don't come back from. The typical response would be move on from fighting and scrounge for other options to make a living. Even that would have been difficult for Jacobs. The doctors actually told him that he would never walk again, let alone box. Fortunately, the man found a winning mindset and stuck to it.

"I looked at Cancer as just another opponent," Jacobs said. "Boxing teaches you to look at everything as a fight, and you prepare for the fight appropriately."

He turned one of the lowest moments in his life into a

surprise offensive, and became world champion after less than two years being cancer-free.

This was how Jacobs graduated from simply being a compelling human-interest story. He refused to become the tale of a gifted, young athlete who nearly had his career and life snuffed out by bone cancer. Instead, he became genuinely important boxing story.

The night he went the distance with Gennady Golovkin at Madison Square Garden, he took Golokovin the full twelve rounds even though Jacobs was an 8-1 underdog. In the end, he lost the match, but won something else. In the eyes of many, he deserved to win the decision over perhaps the most feared boxer in his weight division since Mike Tyson was terrorising 1980s-era heavyweights. Win or lose, that night Jacobs shed the label of "cancer survivor" and assumed the label of "elite middleweight contender." That's quite an upgrade.

If you asked boxing fans leaving the Garden that night which of the two main eventers had the better future prospects, the 30-year-old, rapidly rising Jacobs or the 36-year-old and apparently fading Golovkin, the answer would have been obvious. Although he lost the fight, Jacobs won the night.

This wouldn't have happened if Jacobs simply quit when diagnosed with cancer. Just imagine the parallel images: What could have been a man in a wheelchair became a man standing proud, surrounded by thousands of flashing cameras and cheering spectators.

Against all advice and convention, Jacobs decided that he would still press forward with his goals. The illness was transformative for Jacobs. He absorbed the power of a negative situation. It didn't crush him; it charged him up.

If you think it's just sufficient to take advantage of each opportunity that arises in your life, you will fall short of greatness. Anyone sentient can do that. I know, I know. Most people think that if you manage to take advantage of every opportunity, they see that they're doing pretty fucking good. True, but we're not aiming for pretty fucking good; we're shooting for, pardon the language, fucking awesome.

What if we learned to push on precisely at the moment when everyone around you sees disaster and quits. Don't just take opportunties. *Make* them. Become an opportunity factory. It's at the seemingly hopeless moments, when people least expect it, that we can act and pull off a stunning victory.

"I'm a fighter through and through. I don't fear any person and to go inside that ring with a feared mentality, why even go inside the ring?"

~ Daniel Jacobs.

What if we took this attitude and applied to it our lives? If you look at history, many famous martial artists used shocking events to attain their greatness.

Sam Gaiyanghadao had to take a job shovelling dirt and laying bricks. He lived solely on one bag of rice a day before becoming widely renown as the world's greatest Muay Thai fighter.

In 1987, George Foreman famously surprised the boxing

world by announcing a comeback at the age of thirty-eight. Not only was he extremely old by the standards of the day, but he had also been away from the ring for ten years. Many thought his decision to return was a mistake. Foreman insisted that he had returned to prove that age was not a barrier to people achieving their goals. He later said that he wanted to show people that the age of forty is not a "death sentence." You already know the trend of this book, as well as history, so I'm guessing you know how this story ends. I'll say it anyway. Foreman went on to become world champion, again.

Now, let's look at your situation. You always planned to do something. Write a blog. Travel the world. Start a business. Launch a charity. Go back to college. Learn a language. All great ideas, admirable and worthwhile. But then, *something happened.* There's always a "something," isn't there? Some disruptive event like an accident, or tragedy, or flat-out failure. Don't stop moving. Perhaps you've lost your job. Well, great news. Now you have time to learn something new.

You're wasting it feeling sorry for yourself, feeling tired or disappointed. I have sympathy for whatever tough time you're going through, and I'm sure you deserve it. Unfortunately, sympathy isn't what's going to push you to greatness. It's a pillow to lay your head on at night, but what you need is a jetpack.

Sun Tzu, author of *The Art of War*, said, "In the midst of chaos, there is also opportunity." What if you looked for the opportunity instead of looking at the chaos? Yes, it can be hard to look away (like staring at a car accident,) but there are so many better things to see and do (like dialling 9-1-1, in the car crash situation.)

You've most likely heard of pressure points, the mysterious things that ancient kung fu masters use to subvert their opponents with the mere flick of a finger. Or maybe you choose to think of Spock's Vulcan Neck Pinch. However you want to picture it, know that these pressure points are *not* fictional; they exist beyond the human body. They're weaved into the very fabric of your life experience. All of them can be found during difficult times.

Great martial artists look for pressure points. It is bursts of energy directed at their opponent's weaknesses that can break fights wide open. The best fighters press and press and press and then, even when victory seems out of reach, they press once more.

Look at what Danny Jacobs did. He didn't shrink away from a life-threatening illness. He reframed the challenge, and as a result, he triumphed.

Lucky you, there's enough triumph to go around.

5

FEAR OF EVERYTHING

In the final of the Rio Olympics, women's freestyle wrestling championships, 53kg category, Helen Maroulis stepped onto the mat locked eyes with Saori Yoshida. Yoshida, at the time, was the most decorated freestyle wrestler in the history of women's wrestling, winning every major tournament since 1998. These included three Olympic games, four Asian games, and thirteen world championships.

In that moment of eye contact before the bell rang, Maroulis was most likely confronting the unfortunate truth: Yoshida held the competitive record of eighty-nine wins and zero losses. Just imagine for a second what it must have been like for Maroulis to walk out on that wrestling mat in Brazil. She was merely an "up and coming talent." It was an exciting title, but it didn't necessarily suggest her skill and power had reached full potential. She was simply on track to, one day, possibly, make a name for herself in the world of women's freestyle wrestling.

Yet... Maroulis went onto win the match.

Afterwards, Maroulis admitted just how petrified she was. Her explanation was an uncommon, honest look into the mind of an outmatched fighter. She let her mental shields down, and invited us into a more intimate understanding of what she was going through, without the public relations spin.

"I'm afraid. Like, of everything. Afraid of the dark. Afraid of people looking at me. Afraid of being home alone. Afraid of not being enough. Afraid of my fear. Afraid of your impression of me after you read about my fear."

Despite assessing herself as having the constitution of a church mouse, when Maroulis stepped away from the mat that day, she did so as the proud victor in her match against Sauri Yoshida. She was the first American to capture the gold medal in women's wrestling. The victory was not a fluke. Just one year later, she went on to win the 2017 world championship.

But she's afraid of everything, right? She said so herself.

We've discussed the effects that fear can have on a fighter, but there's something different about Maroulis' approach to the problem, isn't there? The most important thing is that she acknowledged her fear. Cladding yourself in thick, mental armour and charging headlong into combat with your anxiety is one approach. It's a good approach, but not the only option. Maroulis found a way to go into that same conflict of the mind unburdened by armour. She simply didn't let her fear stop her from doing what she wanted. It's no accident that she acknowledged her fear, though it's uncommon to do so in such a public fashion.

Let's unpack the metaphor. What do I mean when I say she was unburdened by armour? In her words: "When I pretended to be fearless, I learned I was closing myself off to my creative side. For me, the mat is my canvas.

Without fear, there is no courage, and without courage, there is no creativity. Without any of those, being on the mat just doesn't work."

She used her fear against her opponent, not in a way that made her frantic and aggressive, but a way that elevated her abilities. Maroulis perspective on fear is: It prepares you for battle. It makes you hypersensitive. Looking back on her capture of the Olympic gold medal, she reflected on what the victory meant. Moreover, what all victories mean.

"You don't have to be the best. You just have to be enough. And on that day in Rio, I was enough."

How's that for humble? She reached the pinnacle of her sport, the most prestigious award that an athlete can attain. You would think that makes you officially "the best," right? No, she was just *enough*. Maroulis didn't proclaim that she had attained the ever-elusive state of perfection. She was unburdened with the pressure of seeking out perfection. She was honest with herself, and for bonus points: her fans. This is just one other way of acknowledging her fear.

When we look at something from a new angle and break it down, it loses power over us. Perspective is everything. Fear distracts, debilitates and discourages us. Maroulis knew this, and she was able to use the power of perspective to defeat it. It wasn't some kind of rushing current that she had to fight against. It wasn't an impossible hill that she had to climb. Maroulis simply accepted the existence of her fear, admitted that it contributed to the shape of her world, and worked within those new confines. She and her fear coexisted, somewhat peacefully, (even though wrestling isn't the most serene of sports.)

In life, we often choose the more complicated explanation over the simple one, but this can really fuck us up. We are fearful of life's problems just because it's our perspective that's warped. Remember, a simple shift in perspective can change our reaction entirely. The task, as Maroulis showed, is not to ignore fear. Take what you're afraid of and break it apart. Become a surgeon. Dissect it. Understand it.

I'll say it again because it's important for you to remember. We can choose how we look at things, how we react. That's the thing we have control over.

E + R = O.

Event. Reaction. Outcome.

We, the human element, are what bring perspective into a situation. We can't change the problems we bump up against; that part of the equation is set, but the power of perception can change the appearance of our biggest problems. How we view those problems and what we tell ourselves they mean determines how daunting they will be to overcome. Maroulis knew this. She made fear a part of her story.

Let's break down the wrong perspective. This is the part where you focus entirely on the situation, and not the power you have to change it.

"My girlfriend/boyfriend dumped me."

"The company fired me."

"That guy just said I look like a potato."

Now let's take those same situations and twist the perspective. Adding the letter "I" is a good start. Take a look at your reaction. What is it currently?

"I hate my ex."

"I fucked up royally at work."

"O.M.G. I am so offended right now."

These add an extra element that doesn't inherently exist otherwise. This isn't just about the situation; it's about you and how you relate to that situation. Including yourself in your outlook helps arm you for the battle ahead. So, we've identified your reaction to those events, which gives us a new level of control. The next step is to adjust your reaction.

"I'm getting over my ex.

"I won't fuck up like that again."

"I'm going to keep cool even though I want to crush this fool's head."

Armed with the wrong perspective, we quickly become overwhelmed with something that's actually quite small. So why subject ourselves to torture like that?

The correct perspective has a strange way of cutting adversity down to size. But for whatever personal reasons, we look at things in isolation. We kick ourselves for not closing a client or making it to an important meeting on time. On an individual scale, admittedly, that sucks. We just missed that one opportunity.

Here's the thing, though. Opportunities are like buses. Miss one? Get the next one. Sure, you're going to be late to wherever you're going, but is one missed bus going to destroy your life here on Earth? Only if you let it. Let's not even get into the fact that missing that bus may actually have been dodging a bullet. The next opportunity could be even better. That's getting into prescient, Minority Report style superpowers, though, which sadly will not be covered in this book.

There's an old judo saying.

"Where the head goes, the body will follow."

If our perspective (head) is on point, then our actions (body) will follow suit.

How we conquer fear is how we conquer all negativity. We have this picture in our heads that all winners or successful people are fearless, but it's simply not the case. So, go ahead, admit you're afraid. Let that admission bring you the freedom to go out and do what you want to do.

6

A TIME TO CULTIVATE; A TIME TO FIGHT

A feverish crowd crammed into Kabul's Ghazi stadium. It was loud; the mood was electric. For all the cheering, celebration, and pride of that day, it's strange to think that not quite a decade ago, the Taliban stoned women to death in this place. Now, instead of extremists gathering for a horrific crime against humanity, Afghanistani's were here to celebrate a moment of national pride. It was the Bejing 2008 Olympics, and Rohullah Nikpai had just won the bronze medal in tae kwon do. His win marked Afghanistan's first-ever Olympic medal.

So, who was Rohullah Nikpai? Certainly, his country had devoted endless resources towards making him the ultimate fighting machine in pursuit of a place on the global athletic stage. You might picture something like the massive national undertaking that Russia's Ivan Drago underwent in Rocky IV. Erase that image from your head.

While you're at it, wipe away the glory of Stallone's lonely, awe-inspiring training sequence in a snowy forest. Not only were Nikpai's resources limited, but he also didn't even train fulltime for the competition. Before the 2008 Olympics, Nikpai's official occupation was: hairdresser. For the event itself, he was nothing more than a checkmark on a paper, a number to round out the team.

The single piece of ribbon and metal he won threw Afganistan into a tae kwon do fever. Flash forward four years. It was late, and half of the city stayed up late to watch Nikpai's fights in the 2012 Olympics in London. Instead of Ghazi stadium, picture an ice cream stall with a small television being swarmed on all sides by a crowd of pumped up spectators.

The city was subject to regular power cuts, and when one such cut interrupted the Olympic broadcast, men went streaming out into the streets, seeking lit screens. Restaurants and any other establishment that had a backup generator were suddenly besieged, all for the sake of people wanting to see Nikpai fight.

For those who took to the streets after their TV sets went dark, the mania was worth it. Nikpai once again managed to clinch the bronze.

Let's get back to the original question. Who is Nikpai? His youth defines him. By age eleven, Rohullah Nikpai and his family found themselves in an Iranian refugee camp in the midst of the bloody civil war that gripped Afghanistan. He was a part of the Hazara ethnic minority, which had been subject to intense discrimination from the more dominant groups in Afghanistan. The war only served to exasperate this treatment.

Children tend to latch on to a source of happiness when their existence is a dark one. The most common Hollywood shot is of the little girl clutching her teddy bear in some post-apocalyptic wasteland. Nikpai's teddy bear was martial arts movies. As a pre-teen, he became fascinated with tae kwon do. When he was old enough, he began to compete as part of the Afghan refugee team.

You'd think that ideals like a commitment to training would be lost on a child that's living in a refugee camp. Growing up in a country rife with violence probably comes with higher, more dire priorities, like finding a pocket of safety somewhere in the world. There must have been an insurmountable pile of things to worry about, other than a fun and glorious sport that he saw on TV.

Tae kwon do turned out to be Nikpai's pocket of safety, in a way. The "gym" he trained in was nothing more than a concrete shell of a room. The only "equipment" was a dingy mat and a cheap plastic pad. Nevertheless, young Nikpai proceeded to work out feverishly, every day, for the next few years. He slowly built muscle and stamina. He became more flexible, more focused. You're imagining an epic montage better than Rocky's right now, aren't you? I know. Me too.

That gym work prepared a physically frail but motivated young boy for the uniquely challenging course that no one in his country had ever walked before. It was the start of his journey to not one but two Olympic medals. In many ways, the work prepared him for not just a major athletic achievement, but life itself. As we've said, strength of mind is just as important as strength of body.

And for Nikpai, life threw a lot at him. Growing up, he experienced hatred and discrimination from people due solely to his ethnicity. He experienced the sensation of being unwelcome by simply existing outside. He was beset on all sides by mental daggers, distractions, and things that routinely tried to dampen his self-esteem. Still, he was equipped for it all because of his early training and because he kept at it every single day.

Are you similarly prepared? Nikpai started with a life in terrible shape. I don't want to be presumptuous, but I'm going to guess that your existence isn't as challenged as Nikpai's was. What if things started getting worse, though? Could you actually handle life if things suddenly took a dive?

Nobody is born with an indestructible mindset. The first four years of our lives, the formative years, we're essentially a sponge. I don't just mean that in the sense that we soak up information. Our minds are weak, malleable. (No offence, babies.)

We have to cultivate the strength of mind for ourselves. There's a martial arts concept of a sound mind in a strong body: cultivate mental strength in physical preparations; cultivate physical strength in mental preparations. It's an ecosystem. One feeds the other.

The founder of Aikido, Mashuiro Ueshiba, once wrote that your spirit is your true shield against conflict. This approach goes back to the ancient civilisations, particularly Japan (origin of many martial arts), the British Isles, and ancient Greece (origin of wrestling and Pankration, an ancient form of what we recognise today as MMA). These warrior cultures, from the Spartans to the Samurai to the Celts, all encouraged their warriors to become mentally resilient.

Every bit of what we know about these tribes was developed with the intention to reshape, prepare, and fortify their warriors for the battles and wars to come. In fact, many Spartans saw themselves as mental athletes. From throwing spears to hand to hand combat, they were prepared for it all because of their mental training.

Nitobe Inazo, in writing the code of the samurai (Bushido), wrote that the first objective of samurai education was to build up character. The subtler skills of manners, intelligence, and communication were less important. Intellectual superiority was held in high regard, but a samurai was essentially a man of action. By developing a character in the tough times, we prepare ourselves for anything. It didn't matter for the samurai what their background was - each one could draw upon their character, forged in the fiery depths of whatever difficulty their early lives threw at them.

When Nikpai took home the bronze and became the first man from his country to stand on the Olympic podium, his background as a Hazara refugee ceased to matter to millions of spectators. It still mattered to him, though. It was what prepared him for the fight that gave him his place on the global stage. This is a very important point:

in his youth, Nikpai sidesteps one of the most dangerous pitfalls that people fall into, even as adults. When things get tough, many think, "once things get better, I'll have time and energy to work on myself." We tend to look at our negative circumstances and decide that now is not the time to work towards our goals. We think we need to focus on climbing out of the hole instead of building a tower. Why not do both? While you're down there in that pit of poverty or sorrow, why not take the time to learn about yourself and strengthen your resolve?

In many ways, martial arts prompts us to visualise what it was like for these past warriors. By applying the same principles and philosophy they utilised, we can strengthen ourselves in the good times so that we may cope with the more difficult ones. We protect our fighting spirit so it may protect us in future.

And here we have Nikpai. He shows us that you'll have far better success trying to toughen yourself up than you ever will trying to defang a universe that is—best case scenario—disinterested in your existence. Whether we were born into shitty circumstances like Nikapi, or we are currently experiencing prosperous times, we should always prepare for shit to turn sour. In our own fight, we're in the same position the samurai and spartans were.

No one is born a warrior. No one is born a champion fighter. No one is born with undefeatable belief. This should give you comfort.

The samurai had their armour and swords, you have your inner resilience.

7

MINUS THE MINK

Love him or loathe him, Conor McGregor is known for many things: his meteoric rise to becoming a household name, his unwavering belief in himself, his fashion evolution from bow ties to Gucci mink coats, and his precision striking. The list goes on. No, seriously, it continues. There's his flashy trash talk to his opponents, his knack for insulting entire countries, and some even less savoury things like throwing a dolly at a bus full of people and shattering fan's phones off the ground. Hulk smash.

He's undoubtedly a colourful and controversial figure. You could even argue the man is a cultural movement in and of himself. Whichever side of Team McGregor you fall on, there are some things we can learn from him. Just try to remember that you don't have to wear expensive dead animals to gain something from the smart parts of McGregor's book.

McGregor's most powerful asset, and the one we'll be looking at in-depth, is his ability to distort reality. That's a boldly-worded assessment, but you know what? I'm going to stand by it. When it comes to training, competition, and winning what he wants, Conor Mcgregor is basically Doctor Strange. The guy can warp the very definition of what's possible. He can do this because he believes he can.

Part motivational tactic for himself, part sheer drive and ambition, this belief made him notoriously dismissive of phrases such as "it can't be done" or "it's just not realistic." Many times, when talking about someone who does the impossible despite the conventions of their day, we simply mark it up to dedication, inner strength, or motivation. All of these are good qualities, crucial qualities that you must attain, but that's not how ol' Mystic Mac did it. The easiest way to reshape reality is to reshape yourself. Before you go imagining some distorted human pretzel, let me tell you what our man of the hour did.

Early in life, McGregor worked twelve-hour shifts as an apprentice plumber. The next step in his glorious life was claiming social welfare checks. During these times, he learned that reality was falsely hemmed in by rules and compromises. He was constantly forced to bounce between limitations, performing tasks he didn't want to do, working jobs he didn't care about, and operating on an income that probably felt like wearing a straight jacket. For McGregor, that phase of his life must have acted like a pressure cooker. His insane energy began to build, feeling the edges of his reality and searching for a way to bust the seams.

He learned that he, like many, had been taught as a child what was and wasn't possible. With that realisation, McGregor gained a much more aggressive idea of reality. When he factored in vision and work ethic, much of life could be bent and shaped into what he wanted. He changed the parameters, skewed the battlefield, tilted the pinball table. Ok. What am I talking about? What exactly do I know about bending three dimensions into four? Here come some answers.

McGregor moved around to a few traditional martial arts before embarking on his MMA journey. He had high expectations of combat sports and did not like being told how to throw a particular punch in a *kata* (technique forms in traditional martial arts) or how to move his feet when sparring. His aim was not to learn *the* way to fight, but to learn *all* ways. Here we see his energy expanding, reaching, and feeling out the seams of combat sports reality. Each style had one (or a limited collection of) stances and techniques. McGregor wanted his collection to be infinite. He wanted to move freely and fluidly in any direction whilst maintaining a pressing aggression on his opponents and keeping his attacking options open.

At the time of McGregor's early career, not even MMA world champions were employing this fluid style of movement. For the most part, mixed martial artists weren't particularly mixed when it came to their technique. They were still relatively expert in only one martial art. For instance, a Division One wrestler might have a little bit of Muay Thai, but little else. A fighter with a background in boxing would try to keep the fight standing, because he was best equipped to do battle on his feet. A jiu-jitsu proponent, on the other hand, would bring the fight straight to the ground. The fighters were gifted, dedicated, strong, and on and on. They just weren't very sophisticated.

Traditional martial arts gyms in Ireland, especially at the time of McGregor's rise, didn't think his style (or lack thereof) was technically possible. What McGregor wanted to do wasn't realistic and wouldn't work in an actual fight. Then McGregor's friend invited him to train MMA in SBG Ireland. Coach John Kavanagh was open to all combat styles and experimentation - which gave McGregor the opportunity he desired to start moving any which way he wanted - so long as it worked.

This was McGregor's view of reality at work, pliable and unshakeable at the same time. He was confident in this paradox, but not in the delusional sense. He was confident for the purposes of accomplishing something meaningful. What McGregor realised on top of that was:

many people mistake the limits of aiming high. They see the ceiling as being lower than it actually is.

Aiming high, shooting for the moon, is obviously a solid route to greatness. McGregor realised that there was, for want of a better term, a "true high," and a truly high aim could, if things went his way, create something extraordinary. In his own words: "All that matters is how you see yourself. If you see yourself as the king, with all the belts and everything, and no matter what no one else says, as long as you see that, and really believe in it, then that's what's going to happen."

At the time of his entry into the Ultimate Fighting Championship (UFC,) many felt a world championship was too unrealistic for an Irish competitor to accomplish. Maybe it was, but McGregor simply redefined "realistic" in his own mind. He tweaked reality, and became the first person ever to win two UFC world titles simultaneously.

For most of us, such self-confidence does not come easy. That's totally understandable. So many people in our lives have preached the need to be realistic or conservative or worst of all: to "not rock the boat." This is a gigantic disadvantage when it comes to trying to accomplish something meaningful or big, because although people's self-doubts feel so fucking real to us, they have very little bearing on what is and isn't possible.

Many of us can already see beyond the limiting, conservative aspirations we may have been taught. Maybe you've already learned to aim high, but here's the important thing: take a good look at what you define as "high." Look at what methods you define as "possible." Now get out the magnifying glass. Can these rules be adjusted?

As McGregor quips, "When things are going good, you visualise good things happening, that's easy. What's not easy is when things are going bad [to still visualise good things.]"

Our mindset determines, to an insanely large degree, what we are and are not capable of. In many ways, they determine reality itself. When we believe in problems more than our goals, which will eventually triumph? I won't honour that question with an answer.

For instance, think of how martial arts were born. They started from someone's unique vision and a different approach to the limitations and conventions of combat. These inventive approaches are exactly what created and continue to push the definition of "martial arts" forward. When Jigoro Kano created Judo and demonstrated that a smaller person could defeat a larger one using leverage and gravity, the possibilities of a Jiu-Jitsu fighter at that time were dramatically expanded. That's just one example of reality being remoulded by innovation.

Plug in any other innovator in martial arts in their own time, and the same applies. Choi Hong Hi created tae kwon do, Gichin Funakoshi created shotokan karate, and Mitsuyi Maeda created Brazilian jiu-jitsu. Go further and see what Bruce Lee did for martial arts in general and what Muhammad Ali did for boxing. These were more than trendsetters, they were reality setters, and they didn't even have to wear Gucci mink coats to make their mark on our world.

This is why we shouldn't listen too closely to what other people say (or for that matter, give a single fuck what the voice in our head says.) We'll find ourselves mistakenly ending up accomplishing absolutely nothing, because that's what reality often tells us is possible.

It's so important to be open. McGregor says: "Approach everything with an open mind, with a learning mind. You will never stop learning as long as you keep the mindset that everything works, because everything does work. There's a time and a place for every single move. If you work on it enough, it will work."

Of course, we don't control reality, but our perceptions do influence it. Let's look at the McGregor vs reigning champion Jose Aldo fight for the UFC featherweight title. In the lead up to the fight, McGregor engaged in such intense mental warfare that Aldo refused to even look at him before the fight commenced. Even further, before the opening of the first round, the two fighters refused to touch gloves. Such was the animosity between them.

As the fight started, McGregor took control of the centre of the octagon. When Aldo got within his range, McGregor threw a straight left hand to keep Aldo away.

The punch did not hit its target, but McGregor then followed with a leg kick. That one connected. As Aldo surged forward to counter with a right-left punch combination, McGregor moved backwards and threw a left hook. Both strikes landed, but McGregor's punch connected first. It hit Aldo's chin and rendered him unconscious. As Aldo fell to the ground, McGregor connected with two hammer fists until the referee called it.

The fight lasted thirteen seconds. The knockout was the fastest finish in UFC title fight history. McGregor's insistence on moving fluidly had freely pushed him, once again, past what anyone ever thought possible. Take a deeper look at that fight. McGregor never used the same tactic or move twice in a row. He gained ground, struck upper-body, then lower-body, then yielded ground, then swung wide.

Now, how do we usually approach the task of surmounting the supposedly insurmountable? Chances are, we bitch about. We throw a tantrum. We throw a pity party for ourselves: Why us? How could they?

What's the point? Who do they think I am? How can I even?!

We look for a way out and feel sorry for ourselves. If we're given work on a project we dislike, we're astonished we were dealt such a shitty hand. We fall asleep in our school modules because they're so boring, or we push off a deadline until 24 hours before.

Of course, none of these things affects the actual reality of that task, not in the way that pushing forward can. The genius and innovation of McGregor's style of fighting embody that trait. He pushed through what others thought were hard limitations and, as a result, he created a totally new style of fighting. No one believed he could reach the heights he reached.

He later mustered the same creative force in his lightweight title fight against Eddie Alvarez. His movement was too much for Alvarez, which allowed for a three-punch combo to knock Alvarez out in the second round.

Another word you'll likely hear when talking about McGregor is "obsessed." His coaches say that he is *obsessed* with MMA. Obsession is a powerful ally. McGregor and obsession are close. Like this. (I'm crossing my fingers right now.)

His obsession led him to challenge all-time boxing great Floyd Mayweather in a boxing match. It's an interesting choice, considering what we've just learned about him. He thrives on pushing boundaries, breaking the seams of reality, and changing his parameters. So why step into a ring with significantly more regulations? No kicking allowed, no ground fighting. Why go for it? Ego, maybe... money, possibly... but I think that this was just one more way for McGregor to challenge himself.

When the match was announced, it garnered a whole bunch of comments, mainly about how *unrealistic* it would be for McGregor to win, let alone go more than a couple of rounds. Comedian Frankie Boyle commented: "I think someone trying to beat possibly history's best defensive boxer purely by being a mad cunt is actually beautiful."

McGregor went ten rounds with Mayweather before being defeated. Frankie Boyle was right. It truly is something beautiful for someone to actually show the self-belief that they're capable of, no matter the result.

This is radically different from how we've been taught to act. Be realistic, we're told. Listen to feedback. Play well with others. Compromise. Well, what if the "others" are wrong? What if conventional wisdom is too conservative? What if you're right and they're wrong? There's this all-too-common impulse to complain, hold society's norms in high regard, and then give up on what we want in life.

Don't get me wrong. In trying to redefine the parameters of your world, there will be setbacks. That's par for the course with this line of thinking. Sometimes you try to bend reality, only to have it stay rigid and bend you/break your bones instead. McGregor suffered devastating losses throughout his career. Nate Diaz and Khabib Nurmagomedov both spectacularly submitted him in their fights. That didn't stop McGregor from launching an insanely profitable Whiskey business. He even competed successfully in MMA again after these setbacks. If McGregor can take such lopsided losses in stride (in front of millions of people) and continue forward, then why can't we apply the same mentality to our own lives? Strip away all the ego, trash talk, and pomp, you'd probably be thinking, "fair play to McGregor. He gave them a good run for their money in the fight."

So why not utilise the major principle that drove him upwards to that success? Distort your own reality and fuck what everyone else thinks.

8

ROBOTS AND DAYDREAMS

As a judoka, Zurab Zviadauri was a unique paradox. Born in the mountainous region of Khevsureti, in Georgia, (the one in Eastern Europe, not the American south,) Zviadauri learned early on to veil all emotions when on the mat. The seed of this strategy came from his cousin's insistence on humility and refraining from outwardly celebrating after a victory. That emotional control soon expanded to every facet of Zviadauri's Judo.

No reacting, no getting frustrated with awkward opponents, and no challenging bad refereeing decisions. Certainly, as a Georgian judo player developing on the regional circuit, which meant a lot of matches with Russian opponents, Zviadauri could not afford to show off, celebrate, or be seen as trying too hard.

You can imagine how intimidating it might be to go up against someone with the emotionless demeanour of a machine, but this was not a simple matter of head games and intimidation tactics. Zviadauri's extreme self-control affected far more than his opponents; it improved his technique. Maybe the physicists out there will disagree with me, but emotions are energy. Our voices, our eyes, and our actions are emergency cooling vents for when that energy burns too hot. So, what happens when we lock down the vents?

Zurab Zviadauri happens.

The power of his suppressed emotions was channelled into bold, explosive pickups and counter throws. You might be picturing a warrior body, quivering with the power of compressed rage. Don't. While Zviadauri's face was controlled, his body was loose, fluid, brilliant, and all over the mat. When I say "power," I don't simply mean brute force. I mean overall ability.

For Zurab Zviadauri, this level of emotional control created a nearly unbeatable judo strategy. Thus, our paradox: as a human being, he'd control his emotions, but as a judoka, he was aggressive, dominant, and swift. Let's just say that if his personality and fighting technique traded qualities, he would be a total wimp that you could kill with a sneeze.

He dove for takedowns and created the kind of throws that made other competitors shiver. He was able to do this because he was free, free where it mattered: inside his own head. He was mentally free to do whatever he felt necessary to win.

Other judokas, with the joy of immense state-funded judo programmes, were free in all the wrong places. They were free to celebrate, free to throw tantrums or sigh audibly at refs and opponents. Yet they never seemed to be able to handle the pressure of high-stakes matches the way Zviadauri could. They often mistook Zviadauri as inhuman or robotic. Feelings need an outlet, of course, and Zviadauri deployed them to fuel his explosive speed in his slams, grips, and movement.

What Zviadauri did is not unique to the realms of judo. Just to name another example, Fedor Emelianenko, an MMA fighter, also put on a steely, blank face. Not only did this give him the benefit of explosive technique, but it scared the shit out of some of his opponents. Seeing such a lifeless expression on an opposing fighter must have been like seeing a ghost. This particular ghost is known as one of the pound for pound best MMA fighters ever.

So, let's look past the power benefits for a moment and look a little closer at why this technique is so intimidating. Why does it work? We see people on the street with blank expressions all the time. If the guy bagging our groceries had a blank expression, maybe that would be a little creepy, but it wouldn't be intimidating. In all likelihood, the guy is just daydreaming about what he's going to do after work.

So why the intimidation? It's not just the face, it's the context you see it in. A fighting cage is a place for snarling, grunting, and teeth-gritting, right? So why does this fighter look like he's daydreaming? His lack of expression makes it look like taking you down is just as easy as putting frozen foods and produce in separate bags.

Emenlianko and Zviadauri were masters of this art.

When life takes the fight to us, instead of giving in to frustration, we can redirect it and put it to good use. It can power our actions. Think: water. We've all heard that Bruce Lee quote about the god damn water in the god damn cup, but it's a god damn good principle to live by. Here it is again, in case you haven't memorised it verbatim by now:

"Empty your mind, be formless, shapeless — like water. Now you put water in a cup, it becomes the cup; You put water into a bottle it becomes the bottle; You put it in a teapot it becomes the teapot. Now water can flow, or it can crash."

Now, let's pour water into this chapter and watch it suit our purposes. When a river meets a rock, it doesn't get angry, shout at the rock, and wish rocks didn't exist. It flows around it. Water moves naturally, with efficiency, not with emotions. If you've ever seen water make an angry face or heard it shout profanities, please go to the hospital right now.

Many of us tend to fall to pieces the first sign of adversity. We act out instead of actually acting.

"I'm trying to eat healthy this week but forgot to buy lettuce, so I guess I'll start my diet next Monday. Bring on the McDonalds!"

"Our demo for the client isn't working, cancel everything and fire that damn intern."

"The first publisher turned my book down (fuck you, Harper Collins.) Better throw out my laptop."

But think of a martial artist and their ability to be "in the pocket," "in the zone," "on a streak," or "feelin' it." For them, the seemingly impossible hurdles fall away in the face of that effortless state. The enormous reach advantage of an opponent suddenly collapses in on itself. Every guard pass and counter punch hits its intended target. Fatigue melts away. Those fighters might be stopped from carrying out this grappling technique or that particular striking combo, but not from their goal. They flow around the rock.

For these water-like fighters, external factors influence the path, but not the overall direction: forward. What setbacks in our lives could ever withstand that elegant, fluid, and calm mastery?

We've talked about being loose and flowing, but it's important to make a few distinctions. Keep in mind that in these examples, a fighter's physical state is the equivalent to the actions we take in non-combat endeavours. For a fighter to be physically and mentally loose is actually a weakness under the disguise of "being like water." It takes no talent. It's just undisciplined. The same is true for non-combat struggles. Weak actions and a loose mind won't accomplish anything. Being in that state is a lot like being stoned.

Now, look at the opposite end of the spectrum. What about a fighter that is physically and mentally tight? That's no good either. In the non-combat sense, this is called anxiety, and it doesn't work. If we stay that rigid under the guise of being "disciplined," eventually we snap. Snapping into tiny pieces is no good. Seriously, please don't snap into pieces.

So, what's the sweet spot? For a fighter: physical looseness coupled with mental strength. For our purposes: flexible actions backed by strong determination. That combination is fucking powerful.

That kind of power can drive our opponents and competitors nuts. It's maddening—like we aren't even trying, like we're bagging fruits and cereal at a supermarket checkout. Suddenly, we become immune to all of the external annoyances and limitations that we encounter.

Don't expect this mental strength to come overnight. The next time you run into trouble, you're not going to simply flick a switch and become an android, but you can try. Do that. Then, try again the next time. Practice doesn't make perfect. Perfect practice makes perfect.

If we can become immune to our inner resistance, then we can become immune to all else. Maybe it's confusing to say "be a machine" and "move like water" in the same breath, but think about it. How cool would it be if you could do both?

9

THE GRASS ON THE OTHER SIDE SUCKS

In 1981, Larry Holmes was one of the best boxers in the world. He was also one of the most hated boxers at the time, so, you win some you lose some. Part of Holmes' struggle with his own public image was out of his control. He had been handed a boxing match he could win, and a battle for boxing fans' hearts that he couldn't. Six months before his title defence against one Trevor Berbick, which we'll be analysing in this chapter, Holmes had the terrible misfortune of taking down reigning champion at the time, Muhammed Ali.

Yes, I do mean misfortune, in a way. Ali was arguably the

most popular boxing champion that history has ever seen. So, when Holmes battered and stopped the 38 year-old superstar, he essentially secured himself as a villain for years to come.

Holme's bout with Trevor Berbick, however, held no such anticipation. It was regarded as nothing more than a routine outing, with Berbick a 50-to-1 underdog when the bout was announced. He was a legitimate contender based on a single win, his knockout over former WBA heavyweight champion John Tate yet nobody really considered him as a serious threat to Holmes.

So it was something of a surprise when the fight got off to a lively start as Berbick started to taunt Holmes, walking him down. While Holmes landed the more significant strikes, Berbick kept baiting him, dropping his hands, pointing to his chin and shouting "C'mon, baby!" As the bell rang to end the first round, an irritated Holmes shoved Berbick before walking back to his corner.

There are typically two forms of expectations leading up to any fight. The first is: who will win, and by how much?

The second is: will it be fun to watch? Against all expectations, Holmes vs Berbick was an entertaining and hard-fought battle, but the decision, of course, went to the champion.

"Everybody thought the fight wouldn't go more than a few rounds," observed a smiling challenger. "But now I think the boxing world knows that Trevor Berbick is a fighter to be reckoned with."

What makes these two guys fascinating is not their boxing match in 1981, or their subsequent street fight in 1991. Ok, I know, how can I mention a street fight without a few details? According to Berbick, Holmes had helped turn his second wife against him. The highlight of the bare-knuckle battle was when Holmes leapt from the roof of a parked car to tackle Berbick. Their street fight garnered more views than their televised boxing match.

But no, although events like those make these two fighters exciting in a blockbuster sort of way, it's not what makes them fascinating. The thing we need to learn from is the different paths the men took after the match. At the flashpoint of this divergence, both had their playing fields set almost identically. They both beat boxing legend, Muhammed Ali, both were secure in halls of fame throughout the world, and both earned hundreds of thousands of dollars per fight.

With the kind of financial freedom that we all desire at their disposal, especially after beating Ali, Berbick and Holmes set out on exponentially different courses through life. Until he retired years later, Holmes invested the money he earned from boxing and settled in his hometown of Easton. He employed more than two hundred people through his various business holdings. In 2008, he owned two restaurants, a nightclub, a training facility, an office complex, a snack food bar, and slot machines. The guy even had his own talk show.

Now, let's take a sad stroll over to Berbick's chosen course. He would go on to assault his former business manager, pushing a gun in his mouth. He was also found to have forged his ex-wife's signature to secure a mortgage. Clearly the two boxers had different financial advisors.

In 1992, he was sentenced to four years in jail, though he only served fifteen months. Five years later, he was deported to Jamaica, then fled to Canada. Although he was stripped of his landed immigrant status and tried for non-payment of income tax and falling asleep in court, he was allowed to stay.

Years later, Berbick was found dead after suffering a massive head wound in a Jamaican churchyard, aged 51.

Berbicks ex-wife mentioned that Berbick was obsessed with Holmes, despised him, and was constantly jealous of Holmes' media appearances. Sound familiar? If it does, it's because it's a tale as old as time. The fact that those words can be tied back to *Beauty and the Beast* is apt, in a way. One of these lives is definitely harder to look at than the other. As a side note, I'm surprised as you are that this book now contains a Disney movie reference.

The old tale I'm referring to is a special breed of greed. We're never happy with what we have, but what we want isn't always as simple as "more." Often, we want what others have, too.

Berbick went on to fight way past his prime and took a hell of a lot of damage along the way - most notably getting spectacularly knocked out by a young Mike Tyson. You have to think of the latent energy drained from this man, who died at just 51 in agony and defeat. What could he have done with those years he wasted focusing on what he didn't have? Would he have turned out the way he did if he solely focused on his own achievements and not his enemies? How much more could he have done and accomplished?

We're talking about Berbick because he's not all that he is unique in his behaviour. All of us want more, and too many of us chase it, often to our own undoing.

Why do we do this?

Because of our ego. Our ego leads to envy; it rots our mental state from the inside out. It does a fantastic job of raising up our enemies and whispering in our ears, "you're the one who should be up there on that pedestal." The first thing you should say when you hear that whisper is, "what pedestal?"

Our trouble is, when it comes to pursuits and desires, we can never say no. The million greedy pursuits we pile onto ourselves are just monkeys on our backs. Here comes that wonderful *Fight Club* quote. "We buy things we don't need with money we don't have to impress people we don't like." Our man there isn't just talking about consumerism, he's talking about the human ego. It's a perfect observation for a group of guys that meet on a weekly basis to get their egos pounded into submission. Are their methods healthy? Nope, but they mean well...until they start setting off bombs.

It's time to sit down and think of what's important to you. Without knowing this integral part of your aspirations, success will never be attained, or worse, it won't last. The important thing is that you know what you want and what you don't want. Just imagine the absurdity of someone being an Olympic wrestler but being jealous of an MMA champion. They should probably just pick one. What's your "one?"

Find out why you're after what you're after. Let other people want the life you have, not the opposite. That's true independence, and independence is fucking awesome!

10

THE PANIC BUTTON

A man with a microphone motions to you, shouting out your name, triumphs, and downfalls.

His voice booms. It echoes, conquering the raving mob that surrounds you.

Taking a page from the book of lions in cages, you pace.

A referee beckons you to the centre of the cage.

He beckons someone else, too. Another lion.

You face your opponent, merely six feet between your eyes and theirs.

"Fight hard and fight clean," the referee says. "If you wanna touch gloves, do it now".

Your opponent simply glares at you. Your gloves remain untouched.

You go back to your corner, your opponent to theirs.

"Are you ready?" the referee asks your foe, who nods with fire in their eyes.

"Are you ready?" you're asked.

You nod, grimly, hoping the beast across the cage saw something scary in your eyes, too.

"Let's get it on," the referee shouts as the bell rings.

The fight begins.

The crowd roars.

Your opponent rushes forward, meaning to put their head into your chest and start swinging.

Stop.

This moment, frozen in time, is where we're going to spend this entire chapter. In this second, just before the first contact between fighters, there's one skill that comes to the forefront more than any other in martial arts: The subtle art of not losing your shit and panicking.

When people panic, they throw the game plan out the window. They become deaf to advice. They regress to amateurish actions. They make mistakes they really shouldn't. They just react—not necessarily to the situation they're in, but to the stress hormones that are coursing through their veins.

Welcome to the source of many of our fuckups. You only had to wait until Chapter 10 to find it! Everything is planned perfectly, the Ts are crossed, the Is are dotted, then something goes wrong, and the first thing we do is swap our plan for a grand ol' emotional freak-out, and not just any freak-out. We're talking Britney Spears 2005 level meltdown.

In a cage fight, that kind of freak out is death. It results in taking shins to the face, while half-naked, in front of thousands of people (including your family.) In the cage, panic is suicide.

So, panic has to be trained to extinction, weeded out and incinerated. Like many weaknesses, it does not go down without a fight. Now, what would you rather do: Take the fight to this insane enemy in a controlled environment, or let it find you during the most crucial moment in your day, year, or life? Let's meet someone who decided to fight the urge to panic on his own terms.

Rickson Gracie, son of Helio Gracie from earlier, prizefighter, and Brazilian Jiu-Jitsu superstar, used to get his brothers to roll him up in a carpet and leave him there with nothing but his thoughts and immobilised body. Take a second to put yourself in his shoes, or, his carpet. If you have even the smallest streak of claustrophobia in you, your stomach probably just twitched. If you're a control freak, maybe your jaw clenched. I won't make any assertions there, though. It's your body; you're in control.

This horrible carpet pastime was Rickson's method for ironing out any panic he might experience when being pinned in fights. Believe it or not, flipping out and exploding in all directions is not how you're supposed to get out of a bind. Instead of scrambling and bursting from bottom position (and thereby wasting precious energy), Rickson learned to calm down and think with a clear head in what is undeniably an uncomfortable position.

Whether he knew the proper title or not, Rickson was putting himself through something called "exposure therapy," which works just how it sounds. For instance, by repeatedly exposing someone to tarantula, they can actually get over their arachnophobia. It starts with being in the same room as the tarantula, then sitting close to it, then touching it, then letting it crawl on you.

The absolutely insane thing in Rickson's case is that he was imposing this therapy on himself, and not shying away from it. Slowly, in a graded series of exposures, Rickson relaxed in the carpet's tight space. Indeed, he did it so many times that existing in that place became as natural and familiar as breathing. He kept doing this, every day, until he beat his panic and could stay rolled up in the carpet for as long as he wanted to. He learned to breathe through it and thus, it became comfortable. He never feared being pinned or put in any awkward positions again.

Imagine if you were beaten to a pulp in a fistfight, but had the power to re-live the same fistfight over and over again. After enough cycles, you would have your opponent all figured out, right down to their childhood baggage. You would have moves like Agent Smith, only instead of a cinematic fight scene, you would lay the guy out in five seconds, flat. If only we saw Bill Murray pull stuff like that in *Groundhog Day*.

This is why our ability to recreate unfamiliarity and certain types of fear is so valuable. This is why Rickson made himself into a human taquito so many times. He was studying panic until he knew its every move.

Randy Couture, five-time UFC world champion and first-person over 40 to win an MMA world title, kept his skills sharp by practising with college wrestling teams. The first image in your head might be that of an adult professional busting into a school gym and beating up on a bunch of students. Not the case. This was actually a brilliant move.

By sparring with the up-and-comers, he would keep up to the date on the latest innovations in wrestling.

Compared to the tricks he was picking up from college kids, his opponents were fighting with an outdated playbook. He kept ahead of the latest MMA curve and if he bumped up against a new technique in a fight, he wouldn't be surprised by it and, most importantly, wouldn't panic.

The question is not how technically skilled you are, but how well you can hold your shit together. Panic has a tendency to lock you into hardline thinking, instead of allowing you to stay flexible and adapt. Life is no different. Problems make us emotional, and the only way to survive is to keep them in check.

Randy Couture's head coach, Robert Follis, said, "You have to balance what's physically or technically correct for your fighter with how they emotionally feel about it. When what is 'right' is forced past a fighter's emotional threshold, it quickly becomes the wrong thing".

Don't let the negativity in. Don't let those emotions even get started. Just say, "No, thanks. I can't afford to panic right now. Please make an appointment and come see me later." This is the skill that must be nurtured, so you can focus your energy exclusively on solving problems, rather than reacting to them.

A client's urgent e-mail, "I need this on my desk yesterday." A call from the bank, "Eh kinda overdue the past thirteen months on your loan, buddy." A knock at the door, "There's been an accident at the old mill, call Lassie."

Practice. Prepare for panic, because, guess what?

Time is resuming. The moment is over. You're back in the cage and opponent is rushing towards you, ready to hit you, hard.

How will you react?

11

THE MIND OF NO MIND

All swords are forged in flames. It's a process that you've no doubt seen in movies, sparks flying, hammer swinging, anvil clanging. From that intense and violent process, a gleaming and often elegant weapon is formed.

Like the sword, many martial arts were founded during times of conflict. Be it economic struggles, uncertain times, or open war, the various hammers and anvils of history can be traced forward to things like Bruce Lee movies, *The Matrix,* and this very book.

After a series of tribal wars in Egypt, 3400BC, the world saw its first recorded instance of what we call wrestling today. The earliest depiction of boxing comes from Iraq in the 3rd millennium BC, in the 'Uruk' period, a time when booming temple construction led to a rampant increase in slave labour.

Moving forward through time, we'll find the birth of some more familiar fighting styles. Karate, the Japanese word for "empty hand," was born in the Okinawan Islands in the China Sea as a form of self-defence at a time when weapons were banned by invading Japanese forces.

We've talked a lot about Judo thus far, and I already mentioned that it was founded in Japan, but I didn't mention the cause of this genesis. The style was born in 1882, just as the samurai class was collapsing. Collapse makes a sturdy anvil.

Beginning in 1945, shortly after World War II, new martial arts schools called *kwans* opened in Seoul, South Korea. These schools were established by Korean martial artists with backgrounds in Japanese, Chinese, and Korean martial arts, which would later be grouped as a single martial art: tae kwon do. These are just a few examples of the common denominator of fighting styles throughout the centuries.

The strange thought here is that, most likely, the founders of these fighting styles likely had little awareness that they were in a historically significant time. Why? Because they were too busy existing in the present—actually dealing with the situation at hand. They had no idea if it would get better or worse, they were simply *in it*. They simply had an idea they believed in and a job to do. We can learn from this.

Our understanding of the world of martial arts is all mixed up with mythological Asian ninjas who could shrivel a man's ball sack with chi energy and a karate chop to the neck. This fictional world creates a haze around the lessons that these great innovators of combat have to offer. They put aside the greater troubles of living on this planet and focused on their craft. At least, the good ones must have.

When applied in combat, or even everyday life, the samurai referred to this state as "mushin no shin," which translates to: the mind of no mind. It's acting, not thinking. It's becoming unburdened by your emotions and solely focused on the task set before you.

For how incredibly involved and complex we humans are, the entire animal kingdom has us beat in this department. Unfortunately, we can't discuss this with them first-hand, but at any given moment, dogs are purely focused on food, play, or the safety of their pack (you.) Tigers hunt. Birds sing out for a mate. Cats are dickheads.

The implications of our problems are solely theoretical—they exist in the past and the future. Some clichés stick around because they're too damn true to be forgotten: "live in the moment" is one of them. The more we embrace that immortal phrase, the easier we will find it to face our problems.

There are many simple things that can pull you into the present moment. Walking, exercise, punching another human being in the face during martial arts practice, a tub of ice cream, playing with a dog, petting your serial killer cat—they're a firm reminder of how great the present is. Find the act that works for you. Just don't lean on that ice cream too much.

The sixteenth-century Samurai swordsman Miyamoto Musashi won countless fights against feared opponents, even multiple opponents, in which he was armed only with a wooden sword. In *The Book of Five Rings*, he notes the difference between observing and perceiving. "The perceiving eye is weak," he wrote. "The observing eye is strong." Musashi understood that the observing eye sees a simple truth, whereas the perceiving eye surrounds that truth in a cloud of fiction. Observing is helpful, perceiving is not. If we steady ourselves and hold back our emotions, we can see things as they really are.

Everything about our primal brains tries to compress the space between impression and perception. Think, perceive, act—with only milliseconds between each stage.

A deer or rabbit experiences sudden fear at the threat of an oncoming, bright, and loud *thing*. That primal fear often sends them sprinting directly into the path of the very car that terrified them in the first place.

We don't have to be a deer or rabbit; we can question that impulse. We can disagree with it. We can flick the override switch and examine the threat before we act. This takes strength. It's a muscle that must be developed through tension, just as a sword must be forged in flames. Next time you feel yourself in those flames, use them to your advantage. Sharpen your observing eye.

This is why Musashi and most martial arts practitioners focus on mental training as much as on physical training. Both are important and require equally vigorous exercise and practice.

Famous judoka Yashiro Yamashita had a great mindset going into competition. "My opponent is not as weak as I think; my opponent is not as strong as I think." He aimed to see things as they really were, to prepare his observing eye and blindfold his perceiving eye. Yamashita won four world championships, one Olympic gold medal, countless Japanese nationals, and served as head national judo coach for Japan. Evidently, he knows a thing or two about the art of competitive mindset.

We can utilise Yamashita's mindset for anything that stands in our way. With this version of "mind of no mind," we can shrink our critics, focus on how to get a promotion instead of why we need it, and do one pushup at a time instead of wonder how we'll ever get to fifty. Here's the Shyamalan-style twist ending: once you master your objective thinking, you'll be able to make your subjective thoughts work with you, not against you.

12

A LITTLE TOO ROWDY

Imagine your life and the pursuit of your goals as a complex set of pressure-driven parts. A steam engine is the best example of this. In a locomotive, heat is produced from wood or coal, which heats up a boiler full of water. The water lets off steam, but the gas has nowhere to expand. That pressure is potential energy, and it's used in a controlled fashion to power the complex mechanisation that is capable of pulling twenty tons.

Your body, your life, is a machine. "Talking" and "doing" draw energy from the same boiler. The difference is, one pulls the train, the other just blows the whistle. Blowing that whistle is more expensive than you think. It can cost you your momentum, your progress, and in one historical case: a bantamweight world title.

Ronda "Rowdy" Rousey was the reigning World MMA Champion when she started blowing her whistle a little too hard, and too often. It was 2015, and the Olympic Judo Bronze Medalist had been charged with the task of defending her title from Holly Holm. Rowdy immediately went on the offensive, but not in a productive way.

In interviews leading up to the fight, she criticised Holm's training camp and labelled her a fake. Even if we set aside standards of good sportsmanship, which Rowdy was well beneath, she was also flat-out wrong about her opponent. Holm was a multiple world champion boxer, and on paper the fight was absolutely not one-sided, but that didn't stop Rousey from claiming she could outbox her challenger.

It wasn't just directed verbal attacks, though. Rousey made it a point to announce that she was the greatest pound for pound fighter to ever grace the sport of MMA.

Whether she believed this or not, she also claimed that she could take down undefeated boxing great Floyd Mayweather in sixty seconds flat.

She backed these claims up with facts, facts that probably contributed to her downfall. All of her prior opponents had formulated what they thought were game-winning plans against her, to which Ronda said, "Look how well that turned out for them."

Admittedly, Rousey was working to tap into what truly was a valuable asset. Fans, though not part of the steam-engine system, can act as a tailwind, or perhaps a "downward slope" would be more appropriate to say. Rousey had a talent for catching that tailwind. She was bashful and sweet with her fans, who I'm sure motivated her to strive for greatness.

Flipping that coin around, though, Rousey was straight-up demonic to her opponents. Some fighters employ the tactic of being cold to their opponents pre-match by refusing to shake their hand. It's one of the many head games that can, at times, offer an edge. Rousey had previously defeated an opponent and refused to shake hands *after* the fight had ended, thus adding insult to injury for no real strategic purpose. Despite Rousey's already "trash-talky" history, her offensive publicity campaign was the most vicious she had ever been.

So, we're talking about blowing that train whistle and releasing pressure; there is one extreme version of this that basically means taking an axe to the boiler. Joe Rogan has labelled it, "The Hollywood Trap." Rousey had fallen right into it by appearing in movies and television shows. Later, after Rousey's historic fight, Rogan explained that Rousey had become "So absorbed with this idea. When you're on top, you think you are the fucking person, you are the woman, you're the man, you're the shit. No one's gonna fuck with you. 'I'm just gonna run through this bitch!'"

What we're really talking about here is the double-edged sword of imagination. On the one hand, Rousey's vivid imagination and creativity sowed the seeds of her illustrious judo career, and enabled her to win an Olympic medal, along with two world MMA titles. The mind plays an important role in every fight.

So, with a punctured boiler and an overblown whistle, Rousey's spectacular hype led to crushing failure. She lost via KO in the second round, right around the one-minute mark. This was no lucky swing by Holm, either. Rousey was systematically decimated in what was probably the greatest upset of the year in the sport, and indeed the entire history of women's MMA.

It's clear what happened; her talk got ahead of her training. Those two elements are supposed to walk lockstep with each other. If one trails behind, it should obviously be talk. The disparity between those two things, for Rousey, grew so large that she lost all desire to close the distance. Understanding this state of mind assigns a much stronger meaning to the term, "Getting ahead of yourself."

This brings us, dear reader, to you. There are many, many versions of The Hollywood Trap, and you don't have to live in LA to fall into them. These pitfalls exist for absolutely everyone, from your dear ol' grandmother to that human migraine in your workplace. You know the one.

We're all susceptible to these traps of mindless talk and hype that replace action.

Any martial art, like so many things in life, is hard. It takes going to practice, conditioning, and drilling techniques. Sometimes you need the strength to be the hammer, others times you need the resilience to be the nail.

Now it's time to stand back and take an objective look at life itself. Does the above description of martial arts fit? Maybe you have to swap out some words, but the metaphor is there. Anything valuable that we set out to achieve, whether we're starting a new business or mastering a martial art, can be painfully punishing. Is "talking shit" punishing? Not to you.

Silence is a strength. There's an unattributed quote from Karate that says, "A warriors heart is only as full as his spirit is quiet."

The boxing great, Andre Ward, once set two personal goals that he wanted to accomplish as an athlete: he would win an Olympic gold medal, and he would capture a boxing world title. Do you know who he told? Nobody but his father.

The greatest martial artists don't seek recognition before they train, they don't talk much; they work quietly in a corner. Like them, you must find your corner. Let others step into the limelight. While they're out there dancing, you stick to your corner.

When you finally do talk—you've earned it.

13

LEGO BRICKS

There was little evidence that Georges St-Pierre was destined to become a mixed martial arts world champion, let alone one of the greatest in fighting history. Born and raised in a small farming community in rural Quebec, Canada, he was regularly bullied by older schoolmates. Maybe, one day, bullies will get the memo that they're only strengthening their victims and grooming them for a successful life. Until that day, the world will keep churning out amazing stories like Georges'.

The schoolyard harassment came in a variety of horrible flavours, ranging from teasing and threats to physical abuse and theft. When Georges was in grade three, for example, a bully slammed his head into the table because he wouldn't give up his five dollars lunch money. Yes, bullies actually used to do that; it's not just a movie thing.

By the time Georges was seven years old, his father had introduced him to karate. Soon, the boy's strength and speed started to grow at an exponential rate. He started annihilating bullies left and right, mopping the floors with them and taking back his lunch money, plus interest.

Sorry, that's just the fantasy version.

Although he eventually excelled in the sport, Georges' karate skills didn't help him in the schoolyard. He couldn't stomp on his bully's chest like Bruce Lee or Chuck Norris. He would never enjoy the glorified ego-booster of coming out on top of three opponents at once. It was one thing that the movies didn't get right at all, which made the awakening that much ruder. You can imagine the look on a young boy's face as he walks home from school, bruised and battered, after losing a fight he was sure he could win.

Later, Georges said, "You can do all the karate you want, but when you're eight or nine years old and they're twelve, when you're alone and there's three of them, you can't do anything. That's the reality."

What does that assessment remind you of? Was Georges using his observing eye, or his perceiving eye? He was a master of seeing the world for what it was, without ornamentation, even early on in his life. This perspective would serve him well later in his title fights.

As a child, though, since karate had absolutely no practical purpose in Georges' struggle, it only made sense for him to drop out. It was nothing more than a time-taker and a money pit. Sure, it would give him confidence, but the bullies would just as quickly take it away.

Yet, he didn't quit. Not only did he continue to practise karate, but he also doubled-down on martial arts. To conquer the gaps in karate, he began training in wrestling, Brazilian jiu-jitsu, boxing, and Muay Thai. This was due, in part, to Georges' possession of one of the most powerful weapons a person can have: an idol.

Royce Gracie, so skinny yet so skilled in Brazilian Jiu-Jitsu, held not only Georges' admiration, but that of the whole crowd during the first UFC Championship. They cheered him on wildly as he submitted all of his opponents and eventually became the world champion. In many ways, this strong, confident martial artist was the opposite of Georges. Yet, there was enough similarity to inspire and challenge the young boy that was otherwise weak, beaten on, powerless, and, best-case scenario, ignored.

This put another image in Georges' mind, an image of one great martial artist that could climb above the rest. It wasn't Royce Gracie, though. It was a silhouette, nothing but the outline of a faceless figure. Georges knew that the figure he saw could be him one day. He aspired to fit that image, to fill those shoes, and to become the ideal fighter that he always wanted to be.

Georges knew exactly what he wanted to do with his life and how he was going to do it. One day, he would be a UFC champion. He would invest all of his time and energy in becoming a better version of the martial artist he already was. Every moment, every conversation, every technical drill, was an opportunity for him to improve his fighting. All of it aimed at one goal: to become a world champion. Which he did. Three times.

No, that's not the fantasy version.

So, what's his secret? How did he do it? Resilience certainly played a role, but Georges' climb to the top was all about action. He never stopped taking steps, even if they were small. Every spar he won or lost made him stronger. Every day that he stuck with it made him more determined. He could see through bullies and stare down fear. In struggling with his unfortunate fate as a boy, Georges found he would be successful precisely because of what he'd been through and how he'd reacted to it.

Georges was bullied throughout his childhood and teenage years. That's rough, but in the process of dealing with this reality, he created a far better one—one that could never be taken from him. Yes, swords are forged in flames, but what makes them cut? Action and momentum. Georges discovered that simple truth: Momentum is a fast track to achieving any aspiration, and it is only gained by acting and never stopping.

Unfortunately, that kind of training and dedication is like a fulltime job that doesn't pay off, at least not financially. This just offers yet another example of Georges' pragmatic approach to life. When he wasn't training or at school, he worked as a doorman in nightclubs, or hung off the back of a garbage truck. Just as the world of martial arts provided Georges with a goal, obstruction, and solution, so did his regular life. He treated every day like a math equation: problem and solution. Need money? Work. Does social standing or pride get in the way? No. I've never seen those words printed in any math book.

Once you see the world as it truly is, you can act accordingly. One act is followed by another, and another. Momentum continues to build and there comes a time when the burning desire to press forward becomes so great that you trade the thinking and talking for working. Instead of trying to build a reputation on what you're *going* to do, you become a forward-action machine.

As Greg Jackson, head coach of one of the world's most renown MMA gyms in Albuquerque New Mexico, says, "Your job, with all that mental training and suffering, is just to push your line of breaking so far your opponent can't find it." We do that by building steady momentum towards our goals, piece by piece.

Pulling the trigger on that movement is a huge step forward, but it's not the last step. Action is commonplace - everybody and their granny can take action. A child can do it and so can a chimp. The uncommon, vital version of this step is *focused* action. Everything must be done in light of the bigger aspiration. Step by step, Lego brick by Lego brick, we'll dismantle the opposition that stands before us.

We encounter plenty of simple, mostly physical issues in our daily lives. If you trip and fall, your body's instincts protect you. You extend your hands to break your fall so you don't break your face. If you're put in the cage with a professional MMA fighter, you'll probably go into shock, but you'll still manage to get your arms up around your face. In these circumstances, we don't think, we don't complain, we don't argue. We act.

To paint even the most elaborate and massive murals, sometimes you need to use the finest tipped brush you have. There isn't a much better example of focused action than that.

Our tiniest actions and decisions define us. Whether we choose to drink a glass of water over a soda to save on calories or money, whether we exercise to start our day or smash the snooze button too many times, whether we read to broaden our world view or press "play next episode" on Netflix; we are painting a mural of our true self, defining ourselves one brushstroke at a time. Take a page from Michelangelo's book. Grab a ladder, climb to the top of the Sistine Chapel, and focus on painting the most beautiful mural you've ever seen.

Alternatively, you could splash a bucket of paint on the ceiling and call it art. I don't recommend that approach, though. It's messy, unappealing, and definitely not something that art historians will be talking about five-hundred years later.

14

FIGHT ON YOUR FEET

Farmers were placed relatively high in feudal Japan's class system, above artisans and merchants, but that wasn't the only place you could find them. Commonly, farmers were the subject of stories that contained valuable wisdom. So, before we step into the cage, let's take a moment to observe a proverbial farmer, out in his field, and see what lesson he can teach us.

Like all farmers, this one had a strictly regimented process. While sowing seeds, he would hammer stakes into the soil to help support his infant crops, allowing them to intertwine their stems and grow higher, larger, and healthier. The work was hard, the process was long, but the yield was worth it.

One day, working near the edge of his field, he unwittingly drew close to a rabbit that was hiding in the underbrush. Startled, it ran from its cover to find a safer place. The farmer watched as the rabbit's instinctual fear sent it sprinting, but this time the prey's swift reaction was not advantageous. The rabbit crashed headlong into one of the farmer's stakes with so much momentum that it died on impact.

You probably just cringed at this turn in the story. Let's be honest, we were all hoping the rabbit would survive, at least until the end. For a hard-working farmer, though, the death of a rabbit is not such a sad thing. Dinner would be extra filling that night, thanks to this good fortune, no extra work required.

The next day, he returned to business as usual, with one slight alteration. He hammered in more stakes than usual, hoping another rabbit would dash headlong into one of them, turning itself into a free and delicious dinner. Throughout the day, his eyes were as focused on his crops as they were on the underbrush. Soon, the sun was going down, and no rabbit had emerged.

The next day, the farmer threw even more of his time and focus into his new method of trapping, covering the field in stakes. Once again, no rabbit. Day by day, the farmer laid out hundreds of stakes in the hopes of recreating the delicious stroke of luck that was already becoming a distant memory.

Now, is this a story of resilience, or a cautionary tale? Do the countless stakes in the ground ever pay off? Is rabbit stew on the menu? Absolutely not. In the end, the farmer lost his crop.

What did we learn? Don't quit your day job to go hammer stuff into the ground like a fucking moron, for starters, but let's delve a little deeper into the meaning of this proverb. Now, we're ready to step into the cage and see how the great rabbit hunt pans out for this chapter's fighter.

It's 2012, and Damien Maia, world Brazilian Jiu-Jitsu champion and renown MMA fighter, is just coming off of a unanimous decision loss against future world MMA champion Chris Weidman. Like many of the names contained in this book, Maia's is certainly one that belongs under the "incredible badass" category. So, what went wrong in his match against Weidman?

Maia was known for exclusively committing to the same game plan, every fight. A flurry of fast strikes to close the distance, grab a single leg, takedown, hump leg like a heavy dog and eventually submit his opponent.

It sounds like I'm demeaning his ability, but I'm really not. The guy is a Jiu-Jitsu genius and wizard. On the ground, he could easily frazzle opponents with his skills. The critics would say, "If Maia can close the distance on (insert victim's name here,) he's going to submit him." That claim came with a near 100% certainty, but when Maia came up against Weidman, the distance was never closed. Weidman was the first fighter to really rally for defence against Maia's takedowns and keep the fight standing while picking Maia apart on his feet.

It's a classic striker vs grappler story. The striker wins standing, grappler wins on the ground. Only, Weidman wasn't a striker at all. He was an All-American Division One wrestler who had taken up professional MMA only three years prior. In a typical Weidman fight, he would be the one trying to bring the fight to the ground. For his fight with Maia, though, he adapted.

After that fight, Maia merely chalked this defeat up to size and dropped a weight class for future matches. He then went on a 10 - 3 fight winning streak with the three losses coming from people who managed to keep the fight standing. After these thirteen fights, Maia dropped three more fights in a row. The common denominator? I have faith in you to guess the answer.

Maia's career spanned seventeen years. Yes, for the amount of time it takes a baby to grow up and start driving a car, Maia relied on the same tactic. Most of the time, it worked with very little effort. Perhaps that gave the strategy an addictive quality. Maia stuck to the thing that worked best, but that wasn't the perfect approach. One third of the time, his approach failed him. If Maia focused a little more on his offensive striking, becoming a more well-rounded fighter, could he have been a world champion?

Maia had two shots at that title with a seven-year gap between the first and the second, a gap he could have used to evolve. First, he went up against Anderson Silva as a middleweight, then Tyron Woodley as a welterweight. Still, no rabbit. The reigning champion dictated the pace of the fight. Maia dove unnecessarily for takedowns, out of flow. He looked out of place with his strikes while the champ cruised to victory. Maia later said of his two title fights: "I was just throwing hands knowing that I would close the distance and everything would be alright". Unfortunately for Maia, the distance was never covered.

Take an opposing example: Henry Cejudo. In 2008, he won an Olympic Gold Medal in men's freestyle wrestling. Afterwards, looking for the next challenge, Cejudo began training MMA with plans to compete. In the space of five years from his professional MMA debut, Cejudo was UFC world champion. How did he manage to adapt from wrestling to MMA so quickly? He took striking classes, wrestling classes, and any others that could make him a better fighter. He wasn't just pounding down stakes in the field with the hopes of catching a free MMA championship.

This evolution was seen to full completion in 2018, when he captured the world championship flyweight belt from Demetrious Johnson, one of the most dominant MMA champions in history. Having lost to Johnson before via a lopsided Technical Knock Out, Cejudo's striking was dramatically improved in their second fight

One year later, he fought TJ Dillashaw, the bantamweight champion who had dropped down to Cejudo's weight class for a super fight and in a bid to become a two-weight world champion. Cejudo quickly landed eighteen significant strikes to the head, ending the fight in just thirty-one seconds. Some claim the fight was stopped early, but that doesn't take away from the incredible evolution of Cejudo's striking ability. Imagine the transformation.

The guy was a wrestler, once.

Directly comparing Maia's jiu-jitsu to the farmer's random stake method of trapping would be a disservice. In fact, depending on how you look at it, these two stories are perpendicular to one another. The farmer abandoned his work to become a trapper; the grappler clung too tight to his style to avoid becoming a striker. The intersection of these two stories leads us to one, beautiful word.

Balance.

If you're as good at one thing as Damien Maia was at jiu-jitsu, by all means, go get some rabbits your preferred way, but don't neglect other areas that are integral to reaching your goals. Writers don't rely solely on their descriptive powers, they intertwine moving dialogue and metaphor. Boxers don't just throw jabs, they slip and duck their heads along with meticulous footwork. The gap between grappling and striking is much wider than those two examples, but that doesn't make finding a balance any less important.

But, weren't we just talking about focused action? Why are we now downplaying that focus and learning to spread ourselves out in an even balance? Believe it or not, both strategies work together. Yes, your action must be focused, but picture a laser bouncing off of a hundred mirrors before reaching its destination. Each step of the way, at each bend, there was focus, but the beam still bounced wherever it was needed to reach its destination.

The point is that there's a lot more going on. You're going to be weak in some areas and stronger in others. That's a given, but that doesn't mean you just outright don't develop your weak areas. Eventually, these weak areas will catch up on you.

In Brazilian Jiu-Jitsu, they say there are only three directions in passing an opponent's guard: to the side, over, or under. You're only as strong as your weakest method.

Is your weakest method strong enough?

15

LAZY, OR GENIUS?

By definition, Jigoro Kano was an educator and a visionary. He started his martial arts journey with Jiu-Jitsu as a means to develop his physical strength. Measuring at five feet, two inches tall and weighing only forty-one kilograms, Kano soon added his own ideas to Jiu-Jitsu to even further develop a system of fighting that matched his needs. His additions personified the phrase "maximum efficiency with minimum effort." Soon, this became the maxim of a new style that he founded in 1882, called judo.

By that maxim, Judo and other martial arts are not simply a form of training to fight or an art form, but an appropriately recognised guiding principle that applies to many aspects of life. Kano's goal with Judo was to create a style wherein his opponent would do all the fighting and therefore all of the losing. This outcome was reached as a result of minimum effort coupled with maximum efficiency in technique, footwork, and even breathing.

"Maximum efficiency, minimum effort" teaches us that action has many definitions. It's not always about moving forward or backwards or doing a mix of the Ali shuffle and "Happy Feet" penguin dance around your opponent. It can also be a matter of taking a side-step when your foe rushes forward.

Picture the matador bullfighters in Spain. Their sport is inhumane in many ways, so, fuck them, but there's something to be learned here, so we can't look away. Sometimes you overcome life's problems not by attacking them, but by letting them attack you and then withdrawing.

Significantly weaker compared to the average Japanese person, Kano hoped to teach Judo as opposed to Jiu-

Jitsu because it allowed him to lean into his weakness, exaggerate it in a way that was advantageous to him. As an opponent once put it after fighting Kano, "Trying to fight with Kano was like trying to fight with an empty jacket!"

Naturally, a fierce rivalry sprang up between the traditional Jiu-Jitsu of the time and the new martial art of Judo. The community broke out with frequent tournaments and fights, some regulated and some on the street. The burly stout tactics of Jiu-Jitsu, a style which was nationally used as the fighting style of the Japanese police force at the time, became ineffective against the flowing and relaxed tactics of Judo. In other words, the early Judo competitors would use the power of opposites. In the face of aggression, they would be passive. They would simply give way and use their opponent's strength against itself. This technique exposed some of Jiu-Jitsu's more aggressive moves and attributes as energy-wasters and spectacularly ineffective. At the risk of sounding horribly one-sided here, I should say: lessons from one style of martial art have a tendency to bleed over into others. Not to mention, all styles are in a constant state of evolution and innovation. Eventually, Jiu-Jitsu did adapt to Judo.

One of the more popular developments in present-day Brazilian Jiu-Jitsu tournaments has been coined "The Dead Guard." Anyone can execute the first part of this strategy. Lay flat on your back and do nothing. It's Savasana pose in Yoga, arms out, feet apart. It could also be described as your afternoon nap, only instead of your couch it's on a wrestling mat.

As with many fighting techniques, we can see an example of this technique in the wild. Many deer hunters have been maimed by approaching a motionless, bleeding deer that appears to be dead. If they're not careful, they may find that the animal is still alive. It will then use their close proximity to, well, annihilate them. Granted, that's more an example of "playing dead," than dead guard. With dead guard, your opponent obviously knows you're not a corpse, but many of the advantages still apply.

The idea behind the guard is that your opponent will eventually have to meet you on the ground, and off-balance themselves trying to move you. That is when you counter their movements with a sweep and ascend to the dominant top position. Gordan Ryan, world Jiu-Jitsu champion, used this guard in a few fights, more notably at an invitational tournament, where he employed this dead guard to unsettle his opponent and swing into a heel hook submission to win the match.

Ryan credits the creation of this guard to a training partner, Greg Amici. When asked about the tactics behind what some call a showboating tactic, Amici says, "There is no strategy, I'm 55 years old, my body's broken to pieces, and I need to lie down a lot. I'm thinking of moving from starting on my side to starting on my back, so I can get used to the coffin position. That way I can take my BJJ training into the afterlife with me, since in the not too distant future, I will need it."

Is this really an action, though? You bet it is. Except for that grim coffin joke, this is a straight-faced truth. Nonaction can be action. Yes, it can even be considered our golden ideal: focused action.

As with any martial art worth its salt, we're talking about the fight of the small against the big. Therefore, force cannot be met with force. We can't make ourselves the unmovable object to Newton's unstoppable force. We're are very movable things, as you might have noticed. The good news is, our problems are just as movable.

If you truly feel an issue is truly unconquerable, it's time to get unorthodox. If you can't beat this enemy, you must find some way to use its energy to help yourself in some other way. Like Kano, instead of fighting problems, find a way of making them defeat themselves. Make them unbalanced before you try to take the top position from them. Of course, when pushed, the natural instinct is always to push back. Martial arts teach us that we sometimes have to ignore this impulse. We can't push back, we have to pull until opponents lose their balance. Then, we make our move.

Part of the reason why certain skills often seem so effortless for great masters like Kano and Gordon Ryan is not just because they've mastered the offensive, winning process—they really are doing less than the rest of us, who don't know any better. They choose to exert only calculated force where it will be effective, rather than straining and struggling with pointless attrition tactics.

Take Cody Garbrant vs Dominick Cruz for the UFC world bantamweight championship. Garbrant was tight defensively yet loose in offence. He enjoyed every second of that fight as challenger, using Cruz' forward flurry of strikes against him. Garbrant kept joking with Cruz, each round, and each round, he got happier while Cruz grew tired. Imagine applying this technique to your life: Your struggle, panting with its hands on its knees, and you, standing tall and smiling.

In your worst moments, it's helpful to picture Garbrant: Always calm, always in control, genuinely loving the opportunity to prove himself, and letting his opponent dig his own grave. Your conflict may not be as physically violent as this example, but both problems warrant only one response; A sense of calm.

Yes, sometimes we need to learn from Georges St Pierre and just take action to start our momentum and keep it, but we also have to understand that restraint might be the best action for us to take. Sometimes, you need to have patience and wait for temporary issues to fizzle themselves out. Sometimes a problem needs less of you, not more.

The harder people fought Kano, the sooner they were thrown flat on their backs. The more aggression they applied to Gordan Ryan when playing Dead Guard, the easier they were to knock off balance. The more Cruz flurried, the easier it was for Garbrant to pick him apart. In each passing day of your struggle, you need to analyse your situation and determine which side of these conflicts you're on.

Every fight calls for a different strategy, and some are vastly different from others. Take a look at your fight and ask yourself: Should you be on your feet, or your back?

16

EVERYBODY NEEDS A HYPE MONKEY

Let's dispel a common misconception that sometimes clouds our understanding of martial arts, and possibly this book. Many people think that you must eliminate your ego in order to become a true martial artist. After all, that's how all the great masters in kung-fu movies do it, right? They refuse to fight the villain, even after being pushed, spit on, and insulted. They have no ego to bruise.

Yet, why do we have competitions? Why does the MMA cage even exist? What's with all the shiny golden belts and trophies with tiny kicking action figures on top? If ego is so undesirable, then where do all the awards and cameras come in?

The fact is that ego is a contributing factor in a fighter's determination to compete in tournaments and fights. Totally eliminating the ego, or any other aspect of the human condition, is unhealthy and counterproductive. If your martial arts coach tells you to eradicate all ego - find another dojo and cancel that direct debit in your bank, quick!

Ego is necessary for martial arts and combat sports, just not the chest-thumping, ultimate superiority kind of ego. In a martial arts career, fighters should have a plentiful toolbox of techniques, and one of those techniques is confidence. This little gadget is like ego with tape over its mouth. It's "elite" without the "ism" on the end. These things will only grow out of control if we let them, in which case they can become a big problem.

There are so many inspirational and humble martial artists in the world. One example stands out and above the rest of the crowd, though she would probably never admit it. She walks tall, despite her five-foot, five-inch body. She is MMA fighter Rose Namajuanas. Many fighters protected legacies and eagerly aspired for their place in the MMA Hall of Fame or Pound for Pound rankings, that obsession seemed completely absent in Namajuanas.

The advantages of her checked-ego came sharply into view in November of 2017, at UFC 217. In that fight, she went up against Joanna Jędrzejczyk, the women's strawweight champion at the time.

Rose came in as an underdog against the undefeated champion, but still managed to upset the MMA world when she knocked Joanna down, once with a strike behind the ear and then again with a straight left to her chin. She won the fight by knockout in the very first round.

All of this happened despite (or perhaps because of) Joanna's bullying tactics in the run up to the fight. She pushed hard against Rose on media days and even yelled at her and her husband backstage.

The days preceding the fight were filled with Joanna getting in Rose's face during stare-downs. She made personal attacks, calling Rose "mentally unstable" during a conference call in reference to Rose's family history of mental illness, including her father who had schizophrenia. Joanna even went as far as telling Rose that she would steal her soul and cause her pain.

Steal. Her Soul.

That magic spellcasting probably would have looked pretty cool, but the world never saw the spectacle. Joanna's prophecies were empty, and Rose seemed to know this all along. She was stoic and steely every time the two came together.

When we're being bullied, there's an angry hype-monkey inside of us named "ego" that wants to flare up and rush to our defence. That's no good, but there is something powerful to be tapped into, here. The power of this hype-monkey really lies in what happens when we keep it under control until the moment that we truly need it. Rose took all the shit-talk and blow-ups that her ego craved and channelled them into the severe beating she dished out in 2017.

Former American MMA fighter and current commentator Chael Sonnen says that top-ranked fighters tend to follow a common trajectory. They "mark out for their own gimmick." When the media and fans are reporting that a certain fighter is the next big thing, or that they are a superstar, or they can kill absolutely everyone that's locked in the cage with them, the fighter starts believing their own hype - because that's what ego demands.

Alleged talent and ego go hand in hand. We can even link this message all the way back to Ronda Rousey and the Hollywood Effect. After a fighter gains widespread media attention, they calculate their own importance.

There are almost weekly examples of fighters growing too big for their teams, psychologically speaking. They fall out with their coaches and training partners and move onto the next gym, only for the same thing to happen again down the line.

Even after Rose and Joanna rematched, with Rose again the victor, Joanna said to all women in MMA, "They cannot compare themselves to me. They all are only jealous and talking too much all the time. I'm telling them, bow down. I'm the queen".

For those of us not getting punched in the head every Tuesday, ego becomes a roadblock when we start thinking we're better, that we're special, that our problems and life experiences are so remarkably different from everyone else's that no one could possibly understand. It's an attitude that has sunk so many people, along with great businesses and even greater ideas.

Stipe Miocic is another good example. The guy won the UFC world heavyweight championship and has the record for most title defences in heavyweight MMA history. Despite the fame and money his world championship brought, Miocic still works part-time as a firefighter paramedic in his hometown in Ohio. A typical week following any of his fights, he's back at work. He says, "My day job keeps me grounded. When I show up to work, I'm not some star fighter or anything, I'm just

Stipe. I'm going to keep working in my hometown as long as I can."

Can you imagine being an elite sports athlete and still showing up for work? Even in victory and defeat, Stipe never succumbed to his ego. Ego needs awards and praise and maybe even the high life in order to be validated. The dark truth there is, no matter how much of those things it gets, no matter how blanketed with gold it becomes, no level of success is ever enough.

When it comes to Rose and Stipe, the old idea of selflessness and integrity being weaknesses is laughably disproven. Sure, they're not household names. Some people in the martial arts community might not be able to tell you much about them, but that's kind of the point. Their personalities and flare-ups aren't on the outside, only their achievements.

Do Rose and Stipe care that they're not household names? Doubtful. They got what they came for and worked hard to get it.

If you can find fulfilment in success, without letting your ego throw Hulk-Smashing temper tantrums, you're way ahead of the pack.

17

GETTING PUNCHED
IN THE FACE

Let's set some context for this one. It's the only way to appreciate the coming Kiai Master's fighting record. To recognize greatness, we need to see mediocrity. So, some of the fighters you've met in this book so far:

Rickson Gracie had an official fight record of 10-0.

Georges St-Pierre: 26-2

Larry Holmes: 69-6

Gordon Ryan: 75-5

Ronda Rousey: 12-2

Now, we're ready to behold the record of Japanese Kiai Master, Yanagi Ryuken. There was a time, not long ago, when he held an awe-inspiring 200-0 record in no holds barred fighting.

The questions you want to ask may include: Why doesn't this book start, continue, and end with this man's story? Was he a superhero? What insane bag of tricks and determination can we pick up from this guy?

The truth is, there isn't much that we can pick up from Ryuken. He was more of a one-trick pony. But, still... something that is *that* effective across two hundred fights, even if it's just one simple technique, must be worth writing a book about, right? Surely, if The History Channel runs a program called *Ancient Aliens*, a guy like Ryuken must have his own two-hour nightly time slot, right?

Sadly, this ability cannot be taught. It is as easy to learn as it is for someone to reach out and grab a heavy handful of air. In fact, it is air. Ryuken defeated all of his opponents using a silent kiai. In other words, he sharply exhaled upon them.

Yanagi had no need for roundhouse kicks, elbow strikes, or punches, let alone any abhorrent grappling skills. Why bother with strikes when you can suck in *chi* and unleash it in a devastating pulse of air?

Unfortunately, there is one damning secret to Ryuken's majestic career that I must now let you in on. All two hundred of his victories were from fights against his own students. There are videos of such fights, some of which are on par with Uma Therman beating up eighty-eight dudes in *Kill Bill,* or Neo knocking down a dense flock of Agent Smiths in *Matrix Reloaded.*

Countless students charge into the fray against their lone master as he repeatedly deflects their attacks, then literally blows them down. Some of the students are actually armed, yet Ryuken emerges without a scratch. What's really crazy about this is that Ryuken wasn't simply putting on a show for the sake of gaining students and money. He truly believed in his ability.

Ryuken must have felt as though he was the baddest motherfucker on Earth, despite his theories clearly originating from another planet. In fact, he had such confidence in his abilities to literally blow his opponents down that he issued a public challenge: Five thousand US dollars to anyone who could beat him in a fight.

MMA fighter Tsuyoshi Iwakura graciously answered the call. I don't need to tell you that the fight was a short one. Ryuken came out slowly waving his arms around, while Iwakura held back for a moment, studying the bizarre collection of discipline and insanity. Eventually, though, enough was enough, and Ryuken came in with a knee to the sternum and a left hook that dropped Ryuken to his knees.

Being that this fight took place in Ryuken's own academy, the bulk of the crowd murmured in disbelief. Tsuyoshi Iwakura stepped back and extended a staying hand, checking and double-checking that Ryuken was okay. The power of human belief, or perhaps hard-headedness, was exemplified on that day when Ryuken, clutching a bleeding nose, decided to go for another round.

Maybe we should stop the story there. Although there is some satisfaction that comes from the idea of a fake martial artist being put in his place, we are still talking about an old man getting laid out by a younger, more adept fighter. The circle of fault and victimisation makes more than a few rotations in this utterly bizarre affair.

Perhaps some shame belongs to Iwakura for accepting the fight in the first place. Although he respectfully held back after the first knock-down, he slightly vilified himself by the relentless strikes that brought the second round to a close. Yet, someone had to accept the challenge to expose the truth, right?

Then there's Ryuken, who was only working within the parameters of his own misguided beliefs. Many people fall victim to this, but then again, he *did* put a rather egotistical $5000 prize on his own head. Or did ego have nothing to do with it? Was his plan simply to bring magic into the world?

Then there are his students. A psychologist could probably write a whole bookshelf on whatever human behaviour caused those kids to go along with their master's narrative. Many if not all of them seemed to truly believe that they were being knocked down by their master's breath. Perhaps it was their intense desire to live in a fantastical world that sent Ryuken's face on a collision course with Iwakura's fist. If two hundred people crumbled at your feet every time you sneezed, what kind of conclusions would you draw?

"Sneeze less," probably.

We're not here to place the blame, though. We're here to learn from the mistakes and triumphs of others. So, we must take our leave from this somewhat gut-wrenching fight and find our lesson in the aftermath.

Surely the myth of blowing sharply into your opponent's face as a means of self-defence was busted, yes? No. Apart from handing over possibly the easiest payday in the history of fighting, Ryuken and his students refused to accept defeat. Yes, he still had students.

Ryuken and his students continued to believe that theirs was the truest and most effective fighting style. Officially, Ryuken puts his loss down to two possibilities: Either Iwakura redirected his chi against him, or Iwakura unknowingly possessed equally strong, "counter-chi." The Kiai master no doubt had a glass jaw, but he also had a pretty hard head. Welcome to this chapter's lesson.

You have to endeavour to eliminate what doesn't work.

We're all going to get reality checked at some point in our lives. There's a quote attributed to the no holds barred fighting style, Vale Tudo: "Everyone has a plan until they get punched in the face." Almost without a doubt, your punch is coming.

Murphy's Law dictates that what can go wrong will go wrong. For our purposes, Murphy is your Iwakura. He is waiting for you, somewhere, ready to come knock you out at any moment. He might even be right behind you, arm cocked, moments from sucker-punching the breath right out of you.

A reality check is inevitable. Murphy doesn't give a shit whether we've taken ownership of our reactions, learned to solely focus on matters within our control, practised co-existing with our emotions, or minimised our ego. You can embody every page of this book (stripping away the parts that don't work for you, of course) and still... here comes Murphy. No matter how mature and correct your approach may be, you must be ready for a reality check.

As we start moving towards our goals, it's natural for them to shift around following these reality checks. So many people spend so much of their lives chasing goals that they don't truly desire because "winners don't quit," or some bullshit like that.

It's important not to struggle for rigid goals. Don't cave in at the first sign of difficulty, but fall in love with the process of doing work towards your ever-evolving goals. Coach John Kavanagh says, "If a loss, a setback, a failure, or a refusal was enough to put you off your passion, then it was never your passion."

Remember this: The ultimate goal is not the end result, but the person you become in pursuit of that goal.

Identify and pursue your passions and the person that you want to be.

Perhaps you're struggling to pursue your goals right now. We just have to try to identify what isn't working, and rectify it. What's your version of blowing in your opponent's face? Maybe stop doing that.

This doesn't mean that you should start all over again when a setback happens. Reality checks happen. Life goals change. Priorities change. Don't abandon goals, but rather, build upon them to create better ones that serve the updated version of yourself.

Identifying what *isn't* serving you is the hardest part. It's easy to be bitter, like Ryuken, to hate even the thought of your martial art being utterly useless as a form of self-defence, to despise fighting champions who genuinely fought, to insist that you could knock someone out with your breath.

Picture the classic line graph that's used to show projections of future profits, population, or the global climate. It starts low on the left, travels up through the past, and branches off to when it reaches the future, on the right. The further in the future the projection displays, the wider the potential. The prediction becomes less accurate as time goes on.

The right side of this graph, where that expanding line hits the end, that is your goal. Its location will change. The only thing that you have to be sure of is that every time your trajectory changes, the line gets thinner. Your focus increases and your projection becomes narrower.

"Say little, do much."

It's a great and old saying that has managed to stick around for a few reasons. It's catchy, and it's effective. The "much" in this case is variable. Try one approach. then another, then another. Bin the ones that fail, no matter how emotionally appealing they are.

18
NO MONEY, NO PROBLEM

The media has dubbed Lucia Rijker as the most dangerous woman in the world. You may be wondering: "How do I earn a title like *THAT*?" Let's take a quick look at this warrior's youthful origin story. I promise it's shorter and better than Darth Vader's childhood in *Phantom Menace*.

She was born in the Netherlands in 1967. She began her foray into combat sports at age six. Nine years later, at age fifteen, she knocked out the reigning American Kickboxing Champion, Lilly Rodriguez, who was 12 years older than her.

There. I told you it was short. No Jar Jar Binks required.

The real story, of course, takes place in the years that immediately follow her prodigious victory. Despite the scope of her accomplishment, there was no clear way for Rijker to make a living doing what she loved. It was the 1980s, and there simply weren't enough professional women kickboxers or boxers to compete against, let alone interest in the sport. Even for that fight against Rodriguez, she was offered a measly $25 by the promoter. Pretty small money, even for forty years ago.

The phrase, "It's not about the money," gets used quite a bit, often probably as a total lie. I'm not sure if Rijker ever used those words, but she certainly portrayed them with her actions. She kept fighting after she earned those $25, and eventually amassed a 36-0 (25 KO) record as a kickboxer and won four different world titles, as well as a 17-0 (14 KO) boxing record.

Post fighting, Rijker appeared in numerous movies and TV shows, and even hosted a show of her own. None of these high pay-outs would have been possible had she quit fighting because it didn't earn her a living. She persisted in her passion, but allowed her vision to change, subtly. Sound familiar? She was a kickboxer by trade, but when boxing opportunities came along, she changed tact. Something was driving her, and I'm pretty sure it was more than the word "boxing" being in both combat sports. She simply loved to fight, and most likely loved to win.

That's what people who defy the odds do. Persist, but don't resist. That's how people become great at what they do. Whether it's knocking people out flat or blowing through gender stereotypes, they start anywhere, anyhow, and press forward. It sounds like a paradox, but in order to get the money, Rijker had to fight like she was already rich.

The greats don't care if the conditions aren't perfect or if they're being slighted, because they know if they persist just a little bit, if they can just get some momentum, they can make it work. So it went for Lucia Rijker. Nowadays, she's still in the conversation as the most dangerous woman in the world, even though her last fight was in 2004 and women's MMA has since exploded onto the scene, unleashing a slew of other contenders for her unofficial title.

Would we still be talking about her today if she had turned up her nose at that measly offer by the fight promotor in 1982? It's possible. After all, she is one hell of a fighter, but chances are it would have taken longer, not happened or all, or she wouldn't have soared as high as she did. One thing is certain, though, none of it could have happened if she'd stopped after that first kickboxing fight.

So, the first step is to get into a fighting stance and throw out a jab or a front kick. Let's say you've already done that. Fantastic. Good job with the jab. Nice kick. You're already ahead of most people who just stand, arms at their sides, imagining how cool it would be if they could pin the fighter in front of them.

After that first strike, let's ask an honest question: Could you be doing more?

You see, persistence is the difference between those who made it happen and those still in training. Even those that are in training and making zero progress are way ahead of the people sitting at home watching a fight on TV and telling their family and friends that they could've been a contender. Take Mackenzie Dern, for instance. Like all of us, she has days when she feels like skipping a training session. Her trick? When she feels this slump, she conjures up a mental picture of some future opponent training harder than her, sweating more than her, and showing more dedication than her. Since Dern is a multiple-time world champion in Brazilian Jiu-Jitsu and professional MMA fighter, we can assume that this type of dedication takes people places.

So go the sayings.

"No pain, no gain."

"No triumph without toil."

"No rose without thorns."

"No life without strife."

"No, seriously, get up and keep fighting, you idiot."

Right now, if some big brute knocked you down and pinned you to the ground, how would you respond? For this lesson's sake, first, let's say you panic (because you haven't spent enough time rolled up in a carpet like Rickson Gracie.) You push with all your strength to get him off of you. This guy is big, though. Just using his body weight, he's able to keep your shoulders down. If anything, the harder you push up against him, the harder you're pushing yourself into the ground. If you want, you can keep pushing and struggling until your past the point of exhaustion. That's persistence, right? Pushing and pushing until something gives? Kind of, but that's not the type of persistence we're talking about.

There is a much easier way. First, you don't panic. (Stop. Carpet time.) Don't do anything stupid like give up a straight arm and get it broken or expose your neck and get choked the fuck out. You're about to get into a car crash, do you try to slam the car into reverse, or slow it down first? The same mechanic applies here. First you work to get on your side. We're not trying to leap back onto our feet in one move. This is a war of attrition. Finally, from your side, you can start to break down this guy's hold on you. Slowly but surely.

Lucia Rijker's career over boxing and kickboxing totalled twenty-two years. If we hope to overcome the mountains of shit we have to contend with, we'd do well to think about Rijker. With her help, we can solidify our determination with or without money. We will not be overwhelmed because it hasn't been done before. We will not be rushed in pursuit of becoming who we want to become. We will hack and claw away at this mountain until a way over, under, or through is forged. Our message to our troubles can be adapted from *Star Trek's* Borg: Resistance is futile.

The beauty of Reijker's determination is not just that it earned her the title of "Most likely to kill you." By going against the traditional male-dominated combat sports at the time, she paved the way for something entirely new: Women in combat sports. She could not have done that had she not persisted in her passion.

Don't think of Rijker's story as the exception to the rule - it should be the rule.

Take another example: Adam Wheeler had a single win and fifteen losses in his high school freshman year wrestling tournaments. Fifteen losses! Fast forward eight years, and he's an Olympic Bronze medallist for USA in Greco Roman Wrestling. Fast forward another six years, and he's a Brazilian Jiu-Jitsu black belt and a World Jiu-Jitsu Master Champion.

"Overnight success" is something that takes longer than people think. (Hint: Longer than one night.) The phrase is often just persistence in disguise. There's an old Brazilian Jiu-Jitsu saying: "A black belt is simply a white belt who didn't quit."

As usual, though, Muhammad Ali wins for his phrasing of this idea. He once said that it isn't the mountains ahead that wear you out. It's the pebble in your shoe. Get rid of that pebble, shake out your shoes, and accept the fact that the mountain isn't going anywhere.

Too many people assume that successes like Rijker's and Wheeler's came from a flash of insight, that they cracked their problem with pure unfiltered "talent".

Working at goals...works. It's that simple, (but not easy.)

Did Rijker knock out Rodriguez in just one night? Well, yeah, but remember: She had been preparing for that fight since she was six years old.

When you fight all the way to the bell, there's no reason to worry about the clock. You know that every second available is yours to use. So, temporary setbacks aren't going to knock you off course. They're just bumps along a long road that you intend to travel.

Don't think about winning. Think about this drill, this next move, the task at hand. In the chaos of martial arts, persistence provides a way to greatness. If we break things down into pieces and take it one step at a time, eventually the pieces will fall perfectly into place.

...OK, that made it sound a little too easy. The pieces won't fall into place, but fuck it, you'll certainly lift, set, and cement every last one of them.

19

THE MYTH OF MASTERY

Diego Sanchez isn't one of the greatest MMA fighters of all time. He hasn't even been a title contender since 2009. That's over ten years without even a vague promise of fighting for a gold belt, let alone actually holding one in his bare hands. He has had a total of thirty-nine professional MMA fights, twenty of which have gone to the judge's scorecards. He has spent over seven hours in a cage, fighting, throughout his career. Is he brain-damaged? Possibly, but that's not necessarily what makes him keep getting back into the cage.

Sanchez once said, "I look at a motorbike like it's an iron horse, a living thing that you have to build a relationship with." What does this tell us about Sanchez? Apart from sounding like he's trying to feed a motorbike oats or something, it indicates a healthy attitude towards his goals. Instead of something that needs to be conquered or completed, it's a relationship that needs to be achieved and maintained. There is no end to the process, just an endless stairway of learning.

So, does he love to fight? Absolutely. Yes. This is a person who could do without the fame, the glory, or even the high-end pay-outs that fighting can offer him. The dude just loves to fight. As you might have noticed, we're still in the realm of: "It's not about the money." Let's dive a little deeper and see what Sanchez' version of that philosophy has to offer us.

In the early days of MMA, the UFC was in heavy debt and struggling to push the sport out to wider audiences in North America. MMA was still only something you saw on VHS tapes and DVDs, which would be traded and passed around among friends. When the few major events happened, you pitched in on a pay-per-view or went in search of some bar with a Chuck Liddell poster hastily taped to the wall.

If you happened to meet another MMA fan, it was the best day of your life. Okay, maybe I'm exaggerating a little. The point is, MMA was in its infancy, and it needed help to grow.

So, when a relatively new cable network starting running ads promising a weekly MMA show, it was almost like a holiday for existing fans. Here was this fringe sport being wrapped up in the warm embrace of reality TV, which at the time was an immediately recognisable and respected form of entertainment.

Here, it seemed, was the introduction MMA had been waiting for: A martial arts tournament disguised as a game show, with plenty of the "strangers-in-a-house" drama, which was a staple of the form. And at the centre of it? Crazy ol' Diego Sanchez. I really mean crazy in the greatest way possible. At one point, he ran out into a downpour in order to "harness the power" of the storm.

From the reality TV show, Sanchez went on to win brilliant victories over Nick Diaz, Joe Riggs, and Clay Guida. With just a handful of techniques, he looked like one of those Rockem Sockem Robots, chin tucked into chest, feet rooted in place, and wild looping haymakers that could spell the end of your night if they connected.

More often than not, Sanchez took a lot of punishment over fifteen minutes because he didn't know how to quit. We've talked about the importance of ditching the things that don't work and inventing new ones. At the time, Sanchez' robot moves didn't exactly embody that philosophy, but that's not what we're interested in. His ability to "not quit" despite his strategy's efficacy is the power we're looking to analyse and harness.

So many successful fighters fall prey to all the vices that tend to walk in the door with just a tiny bit of money and fame: Paranoia, selfishness, greed. Those traits hardly existed in Diego Sanchez, which is an important first step to "not quitting."

In his eyes, he was just doing a job. He knew he could do it well, he knew he was right where he should be, and that was enough. Instead of calling for title shots or holding the promoter for ransom to get more money, Sanchez simply got on with the show.

This is a strikingly similar approach to one of Sanchez's training partners and good friends, Donald "Cowboy" Cerrone. With over forty-six professional MMA fights and only one of them for a world championship, Cerrone has said, "There is nothing I love more than being in a throw-down on a Saturday night."

There's that word again: "Love," also known as passion. It's what fuels so many of the great martial artists in this book, but what fuels passion? We're getting there...

This love and passion for fighting is something that both the fighters in question embodied. Neither Sanchez nor Cerrone has ever turned down a fight. They weren't worried about the right time to fight or what critics said about their fighting acumen. That was the external portion of their career, the reaction to their action, the part that was out of their control. Remember our equation?

E + R = O.

Sanchez and Cerrone could win their battles. They could condition themselves for fights to go the full distance.

They could determine their availability for fights. They could not control whether their work in fights was appreciated by fans. It takes two to tango, after all.

Equally, they had no ability to control whether a promoter would give them bonuses, negotiate new contracts, or give them favourable placements on fight cards. Sure, they could negotiate these things, but did they really care enough to do so? Nope.

We're all familiar with the coloured belt ranking system employed by many martial arts. In Brazilian Jiu-Jitsu, it's entirely up to the instructor whether someone gets a belt promotion or not. Let's say you're ready to level up, but you get the big thumbs down. What are you going to do? Quit the whole sport because you want a different colour belt? Or refine your game and continue to learn and grow?

This reality rings true for everyone. What 's so special about Sanchez and Cerrone is that they each accepted what they couldn't control and focussed on what mattered to them: Fighting. Doing what they loved was enough. Any injuries or setbacks can be endured, and any rewards or bonuses are considered extra.

There will always be people who won't give a single fuck what you accomplish. Maybe your parents will never be impressed. Maybe your girlfriend simply won't care. Maybe the audience won't clap. Maybe a 12-year-old kid will tell you to kill yourself on Twitter. We have to be able to bat all of that painful shit to one side. We can't let other's opinions be the thing that motivates us.

Jigoro Kano once said, "Where there is effort, there is accomplishment." That's a worthy viewpoint to adopt. Now, take Count Koma, who taught the Gracies Jiu-Jitsu. That dude just travelled around the USA and Brazil fighting anyone who wanted it. He wasn't overly concerned with the decorations or adoration it would bring him.

Life is not a fairy-tale. You will be unappreciated. You will be sabotaged by assholes. You will experience surprising failures. Your expectations will not be met. You will lose. You will fail.

And that's OK.

But how do you carry on, then? How do you get that love and passion for what you're doing, and once you have it, how do you keep it? In other words: what fuels the fuel?

The desire to learn.

We tend to stay in a comfort zone that ensures us we will never feel stupid. We want to stay where we are never challenged to reconsider what we know. It feels good to be the master of our universe. It's fun to picture ourselves marching around the classroom and drilling our students instead of sitting in a chair and raising our hand.

As Sanchez tells it, "To survive in this sport, you have to constantly evolve, you have to constantly be remaking yourself, because if you don't then your opponents are going to figure you out." We talked about the Rockem Sockem Robot earlier. Did Sanchez eventual expand his repertoire? You bet, and he enjoyed doing it.

Famed Karate Kumite champion Rafael Aghanaev, five-time world and eleven-time European champion, is known to bring something new to each tournament he enters. This could be a new combination he has worked on, a new footwork pattern, or reintroducing an old way to do a new kick. This is why he's so successful in karate fighting. He's always adapting, always evolving, always refining. That can be you, too.

Take Tyson Fury, the self-proclaimed Gypsy King of boxing. He underwent a tumultuous thirty-month spell away from what he loved, during which he battled severe depression, substance abuse, and gained one hundred and forty pounds. Despite that insanely high number (seriously, that's how much some people weigh) and all the other major issues, Fury made a comeback in 2018 against world champion Deontay Wilder. Although the match ended in a draw, many felt Fury did enough to win, especially when he came back after two knockdowns in the last round. Let me clarify: I don't mean "knocked over." I mean completely laid out for six out of the ten seconds he was allowed.

After the fight that night, Fury said, "I just showed the world tonight, everyone suffering with mental health, you can come back, and it can be done. If I can come back from where I've come from, then you can do it too. So, get up, get over it and let's do it. Seek help and let's do it together as a team."

Hell yeah. I want to be on that guy's team.

Let's circle this back to your own personal fuel tank. How do you come back like Fury? Furthermore, how can you prevent yourself from ever falling as hard as Fury did?

Is it a coincidence that mastery can sometimes go hand-in-hand with a loss of passion? Definitely not. Becoming the "master" of something means you're done learning, and if you're not learning, you're just going through the motions that you already learned. The movements become a robotic repetition, which can bore absolutely anyone. How can anyone stay passionate about something like that for long?

By employing a Diego Sanchez mindset: Dusting off whatever shortcomings and forming a loving, long-term relationship with an iron horse named, "Motorbike."

20

TRAINING IN THE MOUNTAINS

There are only three Olympic sports that have elite athletes, who can accurately be described as dangerous motherfuckers. They require patience and determination to excel. They are: judo, boxing, and tae kwon do. There are many other overlapping aspects that these styles share, but we're only here to talk about one of them.

Training camps.

These places are awesome. For each style, typically three months before the World Championships or Olympic games, nations send their first and second selection athletes on a three to five-day training schedule with one purpose: To mix it up with as many different bodies as possible.

There are normally two or three sessions per day, covering a variety of abilities such as conditioning or technique, but at least one of those daily sessions is all about sparring. The talent pool in those sessions is very eclectic. If you attended one of these camps, you could find yourself going up against a second-panel-nobody in one spar, and the very next, a reigning world champion. Of course, for anyone attending a camp like this, calling them a "nobody" is a slight disservice.

The point of these sparring sessions is to prepare for the next big tournament. This is your chance to see how opponents respond to your abilities, test the waters. You're there to see the tells and twitches of future opponents and to get as many rounds in as possible, with as many different styles as possible, to bring your game to the next level.

...And if you lose every single round of sparring in training camp? Nobody cares. That's the beauty of training camps. They're not just for exercise and practice, they're a chance to plunge into a fully realistic simulation of high-stakes competition, only without a screaming crowd or trophy on the line. It's a time to experiment, rub elbows with people you would never fight in a competition, and most of all: It is a time to fail.

There have been tales of many Tae Kwon Do superstars getting bashed around from pillar to post at these camps, only to annihilate their competition when it matters most: At tournaments. Failure, at times, is essential for honing your game. After enough failures, you'll reach what seems like the top, which is exactly when you need to find newer, more inventive ways to fail.

Failure really can be an asset if you're trying to improve, learn, or do something new. It's the prerequisite of nearly all successes in these Olympic sports, other combat sports, and everything we set out to do in life. There's nothing shameful about being wrong, other than the shame we put on ourselves. There's nothing bad about changing tactics.

We should approach these issues like scientists. Any experiment leads to a result, which leads to another experiment, which leads to another result. When testing a theory, there is no "good" or "bad" result. There's just plain old data, raw information that fuels the thought-machine. It's important to remember that, although there are technically no "bad" results in science, there is such a thing as bad research. It is absolutely possible to completely botch a study. That's the part that's in our control. The study aspect is the thing that you need to get right.

The old way of martial arts training where a sensei would train their students in secret, Karate Kid-style, or high up in the mountains certainly makes for great TV, but it has its problems. Both the student and teacher are isolated and insulated from feedback. Sure, lessons will be learned and failures will be had, but none of them will carry the same level of kick as...well, an unexpected kick in the stomach from a new opponent.

This romanticised idea of exclusively secret training reflects a fear of failure and a deeply fragile mentality that is mostly absent in today's combat sports. The Japanese Judo team, for instance, goes on a world tour to compete and train for months at a time, identifying new techniques, trying them out in sparring rounds, and then coming back to reassess game plans and continue working. The Cuban boxing team does the same thing, although some athletes have tried running off while abroad. You take the good with the bad, I suppose.

If a fighter takes the approach of never giving away their "secret techniques" and then flops on fight day at a tournament, all the effort they put into perfecting that technique was wasted. If the technique succeeds, however, no one really knows why or what was responsible for that success. Maybe they got lucky, maybe the opposition was weak. It's impossible to know because, as scientists would put it, the sample size is too small. It was only one test amidst a sea of variables.

The training camp method, on the other hand, embraces failure and feedback. It gets stronger by failure, dropping the techniques that don't work in a live situation that can leave the athlete open to counter techniques. From there, athletes can focus their resources on improving the techniques that actually do work.

In this insanely fast-paced world, it makes sense to view our workflows as training camps. That means changing our relationship with failure. It means trying a new way, failing, and improving. As Daniel Cormier, two-division world MMA champion once said, "You don't quit after you get beat. You pick yourself up, and you start rebuilding to accomplish your goals."

Failure puts you in the corner of a metaphorical boxing ring, and you have to think your way out of. How can you have a breakthrough if there's nothing to break? Everyone loves a good comeback story because it's enthralling to see people go back to the drawing board and find something special. The people in these stories weren't ashamed to fail, and if they did at first, they got over it.

Think of the "Cinderella Man," James Braddock. In 1929, at the peak of Braddock's career in boxing, the stock market in the U.S.A. crashed, and the nation plunged into the Great Depression. As the banks dissolved, Braddock, like so many other millions of Americans, lost everything. With no work available, he struggled to win fights so that he could put food on the table for his wife and three young children. He lost sixteen out of twenty-two fights and eventually shattered his right hand. Finally, at rock bottom, Braddock swallowed his pride, hung up his boxing gloves, and filed for government relief to help support his family.

Then, in 1934, due to a last-minute cancellation, Braddock was given the opportunity to fight John "Corn" Griffin on the under-card fight for that evening's heavyweight championship fight, which was between Max Baer and Primo Carnera. To everyone's amazement, Braddock went on to upset Griffin with a third-round-knockout. As word of Braddock spread, he was given other chances to fight and eventually toppled Max Baer from the world heavyweight championship.

With a new perspective on failing, we take failures less personally and understand they're part of the process. If an investment or a new product pays off, great. If it fails, we're fine, because we're prepared for it. We didn't invest every last cent in that option. ...right? Please tell me we didn't dump the bank into that worthless thing.

Brazilian Jiu-Jitsu innovator John Danaher says, "There is a difference between something catastrophic and something that is uncomfortable. If something is catastrophic (in Brazilian Jiu-Jitsu: breaking your limbs or a choke that's too tight), you tap. If something is uncomfortable, you have to find a way out".

Vasyl Lomachenko, a Ukrainian boxer, lost to Albert Selimov of Russia in the final of the 2007 Boxing World Championships in the featherweight division. A year later, after studying that fight meticulously, he met Selimov again in the opening round of the Olympic games and dismantled him easily. After that fight, he coasted to an Olympic gold medal. I say "coasted," but you know what I mean.

Listen: Failure shows us the way by showing us what isn't the way. It employs the beauty of the process of elimination. As long as you're not the thing that's getting eliminated, failure is your friend.

As the hosts of *MXC* often say, "DON'T. GET. ELIMINATED!

An inevitable question after dealing with a setback is: What's one way to make coping with failure a little easier? The honest answer: Think about just how fragile a grip we have on life. I know. It seems like the opposite of what you need to hear during times of failure, but there's a way to make that fact of our fleeting existence work in your favour.

A man who used to be a nobody by the name of Matt Brown overdosed on heroin in his early twenties and was pronounced clinically dead for two minutes. After that experience, in his words, he "got his shit together" and embarked on a journey of martial arts training. He went on to make a full-blown career out of professional fighting.

It's a story as old as time. Guy nearly dies, takes stock, and emerges from the experience as a completely different, and better, person. The very idea of death can give us power. Fortunately, if we have the right mindset, we don't have to be stabbed or overdose on heroin to tap into this power.

In the Code of the Samurai, we see evidence of this power's existence. Nitobe Inazo writes, "If a warrior is not unattached to life and death, he will be of no use whatsoever. The saying, 'All abilities come from one mind' sounds as though it has to do with sentient matters, but it is, in fact, a matter of being unattached to life and death. With such non-attachment, one can accomplish any feat."

In their training, samurai warriors were encouraged to meditate on the concept of death and accept it. This way, their fear of death was not a looming force in their lives. By realising how tender our grip on life really is, we can begin to shape our decisions, our outlook, and our actions for the better. There's now a sense of urgency, a drive to live each day to its fullest and not worry about temporary failures.

Accepting the idea of inevitable death is a way of turning down the noise of every-day failures. Let's say you assess your failures on a scale of one to ten. Now, if you manage to come to terms with your mortality, that will most likely land somewhere around fifteen or twenty. With that, the scale compresses, and the problems shrink.

If we all kept death in the back of our minds, we wouldn't spend so much time obsessing over useless shit, like bad dates, stubbed toes, and flat tires. All of these are negated by the mere idea of death. One day, you won't be able to go on dates. You won't be able to love, you won't have intact toes, and your car will be in a junkyard. It all goes away, in the end.

It's a cliché question to ask, but let's go for it: What would you change about your life if you found out it was going to end tomorrow? After your answer, whatever it is, you will inevitably comfort yourself with the truth: Thankfully, as far as you know, you have more than twenty-four hours to live.

There's no question about it. Death is the most universal opponent we face. At the very best, we can hope to delay it, and even then, we'll still succumb to it eventually. Yes, it's a dark thought, but if you look that thought in the eye, you will find that there is great peace in knowing this truth.

We can learn, just like the samurai, to come to terms with death. Even our own death can have some benefit. So, how can you possibly let yourself miss the lessons hidden in every failure? How can you not extract at least some value from every kind of problem you bump up against?

Wait—weren't we supposed to be talking about fun stuff like training camps and sparring with the greats? We still are. Right now, we're sparring with the greatest of them all.

EPILOGUE

...and now, we've reached that special part of the movie where the music swells, the sparks fly, and the tears flow. It's time to uncover the wonderful, magical, cheesy, yet somehow universal truth. You've heard it before; here it is again.

"What you needed was in your heart all along."

We're not just living in the information age. We're living in the exploding-brain, constant light show, never-bored age. Everything you want is accessible by way of a small rectangle that you're most likely carrying in your pocket right now. You can pull out that rectangle, type some words, and see exactly what you're looking for. And yet...

You chose to look at this book. Front to back.

I'm not saying this world is going straight to hell because people don't read much more than headlines these days. Media is changing. Our brains are changing with it. There are people today that may never pick up a book beyond the ones that their school forced them to, but they can't be really blamed for that. The river of humanity's changes flows fast and hard. It's difficult to resist.

In some ways, the World has become a great place, full of wonderful distractions and things that help us cope with our humanity. For many, sadly, that coping does not include reading. Whether you think it's healthy or not, the world is becoming an increasingly stimulating place. Newsfeeds and Netflix can keep your eyes open and your neurons firing all night long, whereas books can put some people to sleep ten pages in. And yet...

You read this book.

Don't you see what that means? The cheesy movie line is true. What you need *is* within you. You've got it all under control, and not necessarily because of a single lesson you learned in this book. I know... twist ending. Reading this book won't make you a better person. You're already there, just for trying, just for having that desire to improve.

Don't get me wrong. Hopefully, you've picked up some great tricks and a few role models along the way, but the point is this: You care so much about yourself, you are so interested in improving, you are so determined to grow, that you literally sat still and studied boring, unanimated pages to make that happen.

That's determination. That's drive. That's passion.

Maybe it sounds like I'm giving you over-the-top praise for the simple act of reading a book, but it's more than that. All throughout this learning process, you've had an infinite supply of TV Shows, memes, cat videos, porn, and newsfeeds at your fingertips, but you chose self-improvement. You have the awareness to realise that there's something about your life that needs changing, and you've already put time into those goals.

The reading you're about to complete is exactly the kind of focussed action we've been talking about. You picked a goal and threw resources at it until it was achieved. Now, this phase of your focussed action is coming to an end. What's the next step? Where are you going to point your laser-focused action now? Anywhere. Point your strength in any direction you desire, and you will continue to move forward.

Even then, though, there will be pitfalls.

Some problems may turn out to be impossible to overcome. Some actions are rendered implausible, some opponents impassable. Some things are bigger than you. This is not necessarily a bad thing. Every problem can be beaten in one way or another. I know, we're weaving another paradox here. Just one last one for old-time's sake.

How can you topple the impossible opponent? Simple. If you learn from any failure, you've beaten it. We can use that opportunity to practice a key skill—even if it is just learning to accept that "shit happens," or practising humility.

You might judge a situation accurately, act on it perfectly, and still fail anyway. That's OK. Picture it like this: Nothing can ever prevent you from trying. Ever.

You'll need to control your emotions in these times of failure, but lucky for you, you've now seen that emotions can be managed. In every situation, it is always possible to think clearly, respond creatively. Look for an opening, seize the offensive, and deliver a haymaker to knockout to our problems.

All we have to do in life is just do our best.

Just our best, that's it.

You must be willing to press on, win or lose, and have it within you to be the type of person who tries to get things done with everything you've got. Show your true fighting spirit and be ready to accept whatever verdict the judges' scorecard comes back with, then move on to whatever is next.

Just when you think you've fully put one problem to bed

or defeated one opponent, another emerges, but that's what keeps life interesting. In fact, one of the most comforting things in life is that the world never stops. As you're hopefully starting to see, that's what creates opportunities.

When a martial arts champion is crowned or has successfully defended their title, there is always the next opponent waiting in the wings. Nobody escapes competitive martial arts without losing in some form or another, just like nobody gets out of life alive.

As Frank Mir, world MMA heavyweight champion said, "You know what the true definition of hell is? It's when you die, you get to meet the person you could have been." Mir paints an effective picture there, equal parts upsetting and motivating. Imagine looking in the mirror and seeing the version of you that kept trying long after you gave up. I don't know about you, but I want to be on the right side of that particular mirror.

You're in this for the long-haul, though, not just a couple weeks after finishing "that one motivational book" you read. This is not a sprint. Seeing life like the old Helio

Gracie fights which could go on for hours and not minutes is important. Conserve your energy. Understand that each fight is only one of many and that you can use it to make the next one easier.

As Gichin Funakoshi, founder of Shotokan Karate, said, "The ultimate aim of martial arts lies not in victory nor defeat, but in the perfection of the character of its participants."

We all have our specific goals, but the best of us tie our goals back to the one stated by Funakoshi. If you align yourself with this idea, each time you fail you'll develop strength, wisdom, and perspective. Each time, a little more of the bullshit falls away until all that is left is you. The best version of you.

With that new you, with that increasingly perfect character, you will no longer have to live in fear or be governed by negative emotions. Instead, you will be free to feel excited, cheerful, and eagerly anticipate the next round of the fight. Never rattled. Never hurried. Always hustling and innovating. Always deliberate.

Whatever your struggle is, even if it's simply getting out of bed...

Think of Vinny Pazienza, wearing a halo to support his broken neck in one moment, and beating World Champion Luis Santana the next.

Think of Helio Gracie and his tactful approach to life in which he took any battle he could win, no matter how small. Think of his refusal to take "no" for an answer and the fact that he showed up to practices every day, despite not being allowed to participate in them.

Think of Helen Maroulis acknowledging, accepting, and using the power of her own fear to topple an opponent with an 89-0 record.

Think of Zurab Zviadauri's ability to employ aggression without emotion, to show a face of stone, yet still fight like fire.

In a sense, from this day forward, these fighters and the others mentioned in this book will have your back. You won't see them, but they'll be behind you, pushing you forward in whatever you try to do. If you think of what they accomplished despite whatever life could throw at them, they will help push you out of bed in the morning. They'll put your running shoes on for you and shove you out the door.

They can only do this if you let them. You are the key.

When things are at their darkest, when one event led to a mistake, then a catastrophe, then a personal apocalypse, remember the difficult times in history that produced some of the most elegant and effective martial arts we have today. Don't forget this truth: All swords are forged in flames.

There is no shortcut around those flames, not for you, not for me. I would hope that now, having read this book, you wouldn't take such a trail or bridge if it existed. In fact, burn that bridge to the ground. You've got better things to do.

You've got a sword to forge.

ABOUT THE "AUTHOR"

Despite being a pasty ginger, Adam has somehow managed to survive into his late twenties. He lives with his fiancée in the suburbs of Dublin with numerous rescue animals, including a Staffordshire Bull Terrier named Alfie and two cats that absolutely despise each other. He trains Brazilian Jiu-Jitsu under Coach John Kavanagh and teaches beginner classes at SBG Ireland HQ. Adam is also a black belt in Judo and former international competitor for Ireland.

You can find out more about Adam via his website
www.adamxcorcoran.com
or through social media
@adamxcorcoran

MY GIFT TO YOU

After enduring me for this long, I think you deserve something in return dear Reader!

So...

If you ever find yourself wandering the streets of charming Dublin City (the one in Ireland, not Alabama!) you're more than welcome to train Brazilian Jiu-Jitsu with me in SBG Ireland HQ. Simply present your copy of my book at reception and your first private training session is free! You can even book a time slot via my website www.adamxcorcoran.com. Who knows, we might even grab a pint afterwards!

See you on the mat!

Adam

NOTES

_____
_____
_____
_____
_____
_____
_____
_____
_____
_____
_____
_____
_____
_____
_____
_____
_____
_____
_____
_____

Printed in Great Britain
by Amazon